# Advanced Reviews

"*The Inside-Out Company* is a positive and uplifting read for any individual seeking relatable content for their professional and personal development. Don Manekin brilliantly connects real-world business situations with intimate stories throughout his career, which supports an authentic human-centered philosophy. Unlike most business literature that predictably states best practices, Don shows how the power of relationships and community will lead to ultimate success. If you are interested in making a positive change professionally or personally in your career, I highly recommend reading this book to help inspire you in what you want to achieve."

　　　—Joe Ames, Talent Acquistion Recruiter, Johns Hopkins Applied
　　　　　Physics Laboratory; MBA student, Loyola University Maryland

"*The Inside-Out Company* is a masterpiece, and has so much to offer the whole gamut of business leaders from entrepreneurs to established business leaders still trying to perfect their organizations and get it right. There's so much good wisdom and powerful 'nuggets' here for building and sustaining a purpose-driven organization."

　　　—Ed Brown, Chairman and CEO, Brown Capital Management

"This is an honest and impactful narrative of Donald's journey through life and business with lessons that will resonate for generations to come. Donald balances personal stories that reinforce the ideas and lessons presented, from interactions with individuals across all parts of Baltimore's communities. Seawall's efforts in Baltimore represent the exact type of change that can work as a catalyst in our communities to help people, neighborhoods, local businesses, and the overall city thrive. This book is a presentation of both opportunity and the concept of a business strategy integrated fully with a core value proposition. Seawall's focus on its social value proposition can serve as a model for any individual or organization looking to put people and change first."

— Jon Natelli, Loyola MBA 2016, Assistant Vice President, Global Institutional RFP Editor, T. Rowe Price Associates, Inc.

"The words and methodologies throughout this book provide a new approach to success through inside-out leadership and an unrelenting focus on mission and impact. Donald brings together family, community, and business through deep authenticity. He is not only creating a legacy for his family but also inspiring a new generation of leaders to see their careers as an ongoing quest to realize great achievement, beginning with the power of meaningful relationships."

— Natalie H. Brianas, MBA, Loyola University Maryland; Director, Donor Relations & Stewardship, US Naval Academy Foundation

"For years, I envisioned what the journey of a social entrepreneur would look like. *The Inside-Out Company* not only crystallized that vision for me but also provided a clear roadmap to guide me along the path. The greatest benefit I received was the affirmation that my thoughts and beliefs are not unique. Businesses that balance bottom line thinking and "human-centered" approaches are best positioned to create the impact we desperately need in a capitalist driven society."

— Olusegun Aje, Building Operations Manager T&A Covenant Solutions, LLC; MS Candidate University of Baltimore, Nonprofit Management & Social Entrepreneurship with a Concentration in Global Affairs

# THE INSIDE-OUT COMPANY

## Putting Purpose and People First

Donald A. Manekin

*with*

Asha Myers

Apprentice
House Press
*Loyola University Maryland*

First Edition

Hardcover ISBN: 978-1-62720-318-0
Paperback ISBN: 978-1-62720-319-7
Ebook ISBN: 978-1-62720-320-3

Printed in the United States of America

Design: Elisa Jonas
Promotion plan: Taylor Dacosta


Published by Apprentice House Press

Apprentice House Press
Loyola University Maryland
4501 N. Charles Street
Baltimore, MD 21210
410.617.5265
www.ApprenticeHouse.com
info@ApprenticeHouse.com

*To My Dad, who taught me what's most important by his example. And to our children and their children and the seventh generation to follow.*

# Contents

# Introduction

For fifteen years, the pigeons of Baltimore had called the H.F. Miller and Sons building home. They were thoroughly accustomed to, comfortable in, and content with the decrepit and long-abandoned manufacturing facility. The smashed glass windows made for easy entry and exit, and the graffiti-lined walls offered PG-13 rated chuckles. Long before green buildings were fashionable, these pigeons knew that the small vegetation growing out of the gutters on the roof was quite sustainable. Needles and other drug paraphernalia left a Hansel and Gretel trail to where illicit activities took place both in the building and in the nearby lots.

And then we came. We—my son and business partner, Thibault—weren't there to ruffle feathers in the community. We wanted to work with the communities we hoped to serve and let them take ownership in the process. We believed then, just as we believe now, that as we engage with and listen to others, seeking to understand them on a deep level, we are able to go above and beyond—to give what is possible, not what is expected. By doing this, we trust that as a business, we can make meaningful and lasting impacts on the people and communities we serve, creating ripple effects that will positively affect others for generations to come.

The Miller building was on the corner of a little neighborhood in Baltimore called Remington that had also been overlooked, void of economic developments. Yet, it was rich in history. The community had been a manufacturing center, and residences were built adjacent to the buildings where people worked. The neighborhood was once home to families with parents who sat on front stoops chatting with one another while their children played in the streets. As the twentieth century progressed, many of the manufacturing companies took their business to either the suburbs or offshore, and the families moved out. New residents moved in but lacked the roots of those who preceded them. Decades passed without any investments being made.

Where others saw only a headache and a dead end in Remington, Thibault and I saw a world of possibilities. The Miller building had great bones, magnificent nineteenth-century windows, and a layout to accommodate our vision—residences for young teachers new to Baltimore and office space for nonprofits serving in the education sector. This vision grew as a result of my time as an advisory board member of Teach for America and as the Interim COO for the Baltimore City Public Schools. At the end of the Teach for America board meetings, members would share a "What if?" dream. What if there was a building for new teachers that took the mystery out of where to live? What if it allowed teachers to focus on why they were here? What if it helped them live in a supportive environment and get to know Baltimore over time, so they could buy a house and make Baltimore their permanent home one day? What if? Thibault and I asked ourselves similar what-if questions about nonprofits: What if there was a building that housed nonprofits focused on public education? What if that building allowed their space to be made more efficient and effective? What if their space was designed to meet both their own business flow and allowed for day-to-day collaboration with the other nonprofits housed within?

Although we had what we thought was a good idea, we knew it couldn't be a great idea until we engaged the communities of Remington and neighboring Charles Village in the process. Since the neighbors would be directly impacted by what we developed (and by the people who would eventually reside there), we knew they should be welcomed as key stakeholders in the vision and their input listened to and implemented. The neighbors had a lot of good things to share. We also listened to teachers and nonprofits about layout, amenities, and anything else they had to offer before making any decisions on our design.

Another belief we have at Seawall is that an inside-out company listens first and designs after. The ideas we gleaned from our main stakeholders of the H.F. Miller building showed us how we could go above and beyond for them. The teachers wanted copy machines, a gym, and opportunities to experience Baltimore. The nonprofits wanted a space where they could collaborate with the other organizations there and build relationships. The neighbors wanted a coffee shop that would bring the community together in a fun, casual way. We gave them everything they asked for and then some. We took these stakeholders on tours of the building from its early pigeon and graffiti days all the way through to completion. In the end, they were able to both witness the full transformation, and to also see their fingerprints all over what was built. And because we took time to listen to them, they helped us create a vision beyond that of simply creating great affordable housing for teachers and office space for nonprofits. They showed us how to help reinvigorate a community and bring everyone together under one roof.

The renovation of this one building had a ripple effect that ended up transforming the entire neighborhood, and inspiring similar transformations across Baltimore and other cities.

After the Miller building's success, we developed two more buildings with the same themes in Baltimore and Philadelphia. Later, some established teachers, who had been the very first tenants in the Miller building, let us know they had fallen in love with teaching, with Remington and Baltimore, and asked us if we could build affordable housing in the area that they could buy, not just rent. We had always hoped our affordable for-rent residences would be a launchpad for new teachers to fall in love with their work and to make Baltimore their home. We'd envisioned a revolving door of teachers, that eventually our tenants would move out and find great homes around the city to buy, becoming valuable tax-paying citizens. However, we'd never envisioned developing for-sale housing. In response to the request, and with their input, we ended up developing and reinvigorating thirty vacant "slum lord" houses. We bought ten of the homes from the city for a dollar, and after finally gaining entry and inspecting the premises, we started to realize we probably overpaid. And jokes aside, our efforts inspired the efforts of others, and slowly but surely, Remington had fewer vacant lots and underutilized buildings. The slumlords were moving out. Parents felt safe taking the kids out in strollers and walking their dogs on streets they previously avoided. The community continued to ask us to support their ideas and design developments around their needs. They knew we were all in it together, stakeholders with them in the success of the community. We weren't just one-off developers. Next on their wish list was a community gathering space. Shortly after starting to think about what kind of space that could be, a number of aspiring chefs in Baltimore approached Thibault with an idea. "We have great ideas for food, but we don't have the capital to invest in our own restaurants—you know, the tables and chairs, and waitstaff. But, we really want a launchpad for our culinary creations."

Seawall paired the desires of the Remington community with the desires of the chefs and, with the help of stakeholders, was able to restore an old auto dealership building from the forties into a food hall called R. House. The space allows a dozen chefs to do what they do best, create and serve delicious food, and lets the neighbors and the region's diverse population meet each other and hang out in a vibrant, family friendly, and delicious place. The chefs hadn't wanted to worry about doing dishes or making cocktails; they just wanted to prepare and serve great food. So, R. House has its own crew to take care of greeting guests, clearing, cleaning, and restocking dishes, and Seawall owns a bar in the center of the court to take care of thirst. The space hosts a variety of cuisines like sushi and Mediterranean, fried chicken, salad bowls, and breakfasts, to name a few. R. House is a launchpad for up-and-coming chefs to grow their business and gain a following before opening up their own restaurant in another part of the city. We've already seen some of the chefs go on to do just that.

R. House has not only nurtured a variety of talented local chefs, it has helped continue to put Baltimore's Remington neighborhood on the map.

Remington has become a destination, not just a place to drive through; it's a place to stop and to enjoy and to be a part of something bigger than itself. R House has been a gathering spot for good food, good fun, and good friendships. And even though it's easy to think it's the incredible talents of the chefs that create this amazing experience, there are also unsung heroes behind the scenes working at R. House who value being a part of this dynamic food court and bringing their best to the customers—at all hours of the day and night—to make the project the great success that it is.

Any success that Seawall has enjoyed can truly be linked directly back to the great ideas presented from those within the community, those we work with, and the investors, vendors, and contractors we partner with. Remington is a shining example of how an inside-out company that's focused on relationships over transactions can awaken possibility and exceed expectations a thousand times over. It is a great joy and honor to see the neighborhood improved and thriving as a result of what has been created—and even more, to see a bright future ahead because the Remington community plays a lead role in planning that future.

## Doing Business from the Inside-Out

From my vantage point, the business world today is full of bright and ambitious men and women who know how to hustle and problem solve on the fly. They find solutions, and they get results.

But in all the climbing of ladders and breaking of glass ceilings, and the planning, preparing, and problem-solving, I often wonder if we, in the business world, are missing what is right in front of us? Good and sustainable leadership is all about looking beyond what is expected in order to draw out the extraordinary. This skill is essential not only to be a great businessperson, but also to be a leader and citizen of this world who is able to make a meaningful difference for the communities, colleagues, and clients one works with daily.

Inside-out leadership, therefore, starts with a profound service-based mentality. It's the only way to begin in business and leadership, really. From there, we can build genuine companies that are team-driven and relationship-centered. Why is this important? Because only then can we create truly incredible experiences for our customers by awakening possibilities and exceeding their expectations. In doing these things, we leave a legacy, one that is transformative for future generations and bright with purpose.

This book will explore four paths to becoming an inside-out leader: creating a purposeful company, building relationships, awakening possibility, and leaving legacies. Before we dive into those sections, I'd like to touch briefly on an important characteristic of great leadership—extraordinary potential. It is within you—talents, ideas, and passions that are unique to you. They are gifts that can be shared with the world when you identify them, trust them, and act on them. When you are aware of your extraordinary potential, then you are able to wake up every day and make decisions from a place of extraordinary intention.

And that is precisely the place inside-out leaders must operate from.

My goal with this book is to help you see the incredible leader you already are. When you can see that, then you are well-prepared to help unlock the extraordinary potential in all those around you. Great leadership, therefore, doesn't depend so much on being the best, the sharpest, the smartest, and so on—great leadership, comes from gathering people together to work toward a higher purpose—and that begins by recognizing the strengths inherent in others and an understanding of how to bring a team together to work in concert toward that purpose. Great leadership, I have found, is about having the humility to know who you are and what you don't know, and also about keeping your ears, heart, and mind always open to the ideas of others. My business journey of forty-plus years has taught me that anything great that has ever been accomplished has always come from the collective wisdom and input of others.

What is needed to cultivate your extraordinary potential as an inside-out leader? It's all about vision—about imagining possibilities and seeing beyond what's right in front of you. There's an example I love from the movie *Patch Adams* starring Robin Williams. In one scene, a psychiatric patient jumps in front of Patch and holds up four fingers.

"How many fingers am I holding up?" he asks.

"Four," says Patch.

"You idiot!" the patient fumes and storms off.

Totally taken aback, Patch later visits the patient in his room and finds him busy with a mathematical equation only Einstein had a mind to tackle. More curious than ever about the earlier remark, Patch asks him, "Fingers—what's the answer?" The patient ignores the question and spits out, "Oh, you're just another one of those bright young men that knows all the right answers; is that right? Welcome to real life." Patch takes a chair, and after he repairs the man's leaking paper cup of coffee, the patient—clearly a scientist—turns from his equation and sits in front of him. He holds up four fingers and asks again, "How many do you see?"

"Four," says Patch.

"No, look beyond the fingers. You're focusing on the problem. If you focus on the problem, you can't see the solution. Never focus on the problem. Look at me. How many fingers do you see?"

". . . eight . . ."

"Yes, yes! Eight's a good answer. See what no one else sees. See what everyone else chooses not to see out of fear, conformity, laziness. See the whole world anew each day!"

When we first looked at the Miller Building all that was staring back at us were pigeons, boarded up windows, and graffitied walls. When we looked beyond our four fingers, what we saw was great housing for teachers new to the city and offices for non-profits focused on education. The location was moments from the expressway that connects the city and the county, making for easy access to the major intersecting thoroughfares; and it was in the shadows of Johns Hopkins University. Notwithstanding the decades-long lack of investment in Remington and those who told us not to invest here, we saw and believed in the location's great potential.

It so personifies Max DePree's challenge to leaders in his book *Leading Without Power: Finding Hope in Serving Community*: "We can teach ourselves to see things the way they ARE. Only with vision can we begin to see things the way they CAN BE."

Forty years in real estate, building companies from the ground up, bringing community to the neighborhoods of Columbia and Baltimore, and implementing from the perspective of those we serve have taught me that by thinking and acting from the inside-out, we can uncover the extraordinary potential of each person we interact with, from colleagues in the office to prospects and clients, to the community at large. The magic of life happens when we learn how to understand people on a deep level. Only they can teach us. So, we must be willing to listen deeply and to connect with people where they are at, and only after this, can we begin to develop strategies that are guaranteed to be met with success. This is the basis of what thinking and acting from the inside-out is all about.

Relationships span the entire spectrum of our daily lives and affect those that work with us, as well as our clients, vendors, institutions, and the community. People want to feel connected, seen, and understood—autonomous beings with valuable ideas and the ability to contribute their efforts to a greater good. To support this basic and important human need, the goal of creating a purposeful company is not to work from the top down—or outside in—but from the inside-out. We endeavor to empower everyone around us to feel genuine excitement in their roles. Main motivators are team accomplishments, collaboration, and contribution toward a greater good. Good leadership supports others to perform at high levels by valuing the relationship above all else—especially above monetary goals, which will come as a result but must not be the forethought. When we see beyond spreadsheets and competition, then the business world offers numerous possibilities for social entrepreneurs to do meaningful work and empower communities.

At Seawall, we use real estate solely as a means to an end.

We listen first and leave ego at the door, so we can design and implement projects and services that far exceed client expectations. The mindset of delivering beyond what's possible is instilled and delivered on a daily basis. Those who have come to work with us over the years come because they have a higher calling not tied to bricks and sticks, but to doing work that has meaning, so at the end of the day, they can smile knowing they made a difference.

It is with great joy that I get to share their stories and experiences within the pages of this book.

## How to Use this Book

The book is divided into four paths, as I mentioned above: Creating a Purposeful Company, Building Relationships, Awakening Possibility, and

Leaving Legacies. Within these broad paths are human-centered philosophies and key strategies for weaving inside-out leadership into your own approach to business.

These lessons, learned throughout my entrepreneurial years from other great teachers and mentors, have taken both my business and personal relationships to great levels of fulfillment and impact, and they can be yours as you deem fit. Take from them what you wish. Keep what resonates and toss what doesn't. I have faith you will take what has been presented to new heights of success. Learning to listen and to be fully present with others works both in one's personal life as well as in one's professional life. I hope this book reveals just how much happier and enriching the workplace can be when we live a harmonious inner and outer existence, practicing service-based, inside-out leadership in every moment.

# Preface:
# Getting from There to Here

For more than four decades, I have watched my children and grandchildren walk the beaches and play in the tide pools of Tottman Cove in Maine. From my seat in the Adirondack chair, a mug of coffee in hand, I glow as the memories from those years come flowing gently in just like the changing tide of North Creek. It is for them I write this book, and it is also for every person who dreams of creating the kind of future where they too can sit back and bask in the warm glow of all that has been accomplished.

From where I sit, I know that life never unfolds exactly as one plans, and I also appreciate how that is the beauty of it. The surprising twists and turns of life have the potential to shape us into the capable leaders and compassionate people we are. Each experience—whether trial or triumph—starts to define us, reveal our edges and our possibilities, illuminate more of the path ahead. You might not see where it will eventually lead, but you know enough to keep moving forward. My story, like many others, is a testament to that and, therefore, I hope, an inspiration to anyone else on a journey to build a dream that lasts not only for their lifetime but also into the lifetimes of their children's-children's-children.

In my life, I have experienced great success and a myriad of accomplishments that I also wish for you, and it's not in these things that I boast. It is in the scores of people I have been fortunate to meet, work with, listen to, and be mentored by that make me swell with pride and gratitude. Their wisdom impacted me in ways beyond imagination. They directly contributed to all personal and professional success that I have enjoyed during this life I have had the opportunity to walk.

To understand the book ahead, it's important to first understand how I got here from "there," where I have been, and how that has shaped who I have become.

This is my path in a nutshell: my career began in elementary education, took a surprising dive into real estate when I decided to join my father and his brother's company, Manekin Corporation, then stayed there for twenty-five years before I retired and helped found The Foundation for Rural Education in Maryland. After, I became the interim chief operating officer for the Baltimore City Public Schools before my career finally took one last and unexpected turn back into real estate. Together with my wife Brigitte, we raised four beautiful children during those years, each with unique talents and aspirations. It came as a complete surprise, though, when our eldest son returned from six years of working overseas with a nonprofit and asked to start a new real estate company with me—Seawall Development. And with open arms and gratitude, I said yes! Throughout my career, there were also seasons sprinkled with teaching graduate students—marketing and leasing at Johns Hopkins MIT University and entrepreneurship at Loyola University.

As a kid growing up, I wasn't sure what I wanted to be, but I did know it wasn't real estate.

I was a people person, not a business person. So how did this happen? How did it happen that I ended up in the world of real estate and was actually able to wake up every single day eager and excited to get to work? It had everything to do with learning that relationships overshadow transactions each and every day, and if you invest in those—you can meet with success anywhere in life. Be it real estate, education, engineering, medicine, sales, or fitness—the list is infinite—relationships matter.

In 1946 just after serving in WWII, my father and his brother started a real estate company called Manekin Corporation. I grew up admiring my father's genuine attachment to relationships; he was, first and foremost, an intense listener and a friend to all people.

During the school year when I was young, my father would take me to the office with him on Saturday mornings. I would poke at and play with all the cool technology—rotary phones, typewriters, and adding machines—while my dad organized the week's work, puffing on his pipe, the burley scent of Mixture 79 filling the air. Afterward, we'd stroll down the block for some lunch. Inevitably, my father would bump into someone he knew and invite them to join us. I'd eat my grilled cheese sandwich and watch my father, fascinated by his interest in this other person. No matter who was sitting across from him, my father glued his eyes on them and made them feel like the only person in the world. I liked the way my father didn't rush when he was with people. Sometimes we'd pull into the garage at one of the office buildings the company developed, and we'd be greeted by Lee Douglas, the man who managed the lot and parked the cars. You'd think the two had not seen each other in decades. They greeted each other with a warm smile and a firm handshake. My father listened intently to Lee's every word as they caught up about family and life. There was no such thing as a "hi-how-are-ya" or a "sorry-but-I-really-need-to-get-going." Genuine connections were outside the sphere of time and he always probed for more.

He was truly a gifted people person, yet for some reason, I never made the connection between his ability to make lasting connections with those around him and his success leading a real estate brokerage company. To my mind, real estate equaled crunching numbers and devising spreadsheets. I imagined that being a businessperson meant long hours hunched over a desk, every waking moment consumed by figures and estimates. In this web of insecurity, I told myself I wasn't cut out for that world; I didn't possess the logical brain necessary for the work. At eighteen, I wasn't exactly sure just what I was cut out for, but teaching seemed to be an easy way forward given that I enjoyed people immensely and wanted to make a positive impact in the lives of others.

More by default than by design, I earned a degree in education and would later discover it was the best thing I ever could have done for a successful future in the world of real estate (which I had so adamantly sworn off). My degree laid the foundation for a multitude of opportunities down the road to further educational opportunities for others. My desire to leave a legacy for others, coupled with my belief that education is one of the best ways to invest in the future, truly became the undercurrent of my life's work, as you will learn, even while I worked in real estate development.

I would never have guessed it.

Back in the early 1970s, when I first entered the education sector as a student teacher in Baltimore, male elementary teachers were rare and thus in high demand in schools. I was at once both teacher and mentor and role model to the children in my classroom. I would watch the students walk into the classroom and observe how they each brought with them a world unto themselves-a world that might inspire, encourage, and uplift them in their learning, and for some that could also, and all too often be, preoccupied, distracted, and discouraged in their learning. I could not fix their home life, but I could witness them just as they were. I decided to devote myself to connecting with each youth as an individual, not simply as a student.

Never did my students find me seated behind my desk when they entered the classroom. I was always at the door, ready with a smile and words to pump them up about the day. My intention was always to help them feel at home in the space—a space that was very rightly theirs. With my mentor-teacher by my side, we worked hard to create a safe environment full of positive reinforcement, so the students felt supported and empowered to grow and learn.

Creating this environment was made up of small moments like kneeling beside their desk at their level to work through a problem, making eye contact and giving them my full attention, and above all—listening intently. Showing respect to students was a direct way to show genuine care, and when the students felt cared about, they thrived. Of critical importance to me was that they believed they were capable of tackling any challenge, and if they didn't believe it yet, then they could ride on the energy of my enthusiasm and belief until they did.

Each day ended with some sort of physical acknowledgment of their person and their presence: usually a high five for a job well done. My students left beaming, excited to share their work with classmates and parents, and I left even more convinced in the power of human connections to inspire confidence, success, and happiness. More than anything, I was humbled to have the opportunity to be a positive presence for someone. Because it really is true that just one positive interaction can change a life.

The lessons gained during my short time in the classroom stayed with me my entire life and have become the core of what I came to call inside-out leadership.

It all comes down to connecting with people where they are, creating opportunities for them to grow and succeed, and helping them see beyond the present to what is possible. The work of an inside-out leader is to create learning opportunities in supportive settings. No matter the industry or the business, when leaders lead with sincerity, generosity, and humility for the sole purpose of helping others succeed—their company will also succeed. Empowered people empower people. Empowered employees empower companies. Empowered companies empower communities. It's not rocket science—it's elementary. It's what I learned in the classroom and it's what I later discovered just so happens to work in business too.

A summer internship in the family business first taught me that, and my forty years in real estate only continued to confirm it.

"This is just a placeholder," I told myself when I accepted an internship with the family business. After the spring semester of student teaching, I needed a summer job before entering my final semester of college. Little did I know that this would transform my future. Doing grunt work and running between the maintenance, property management, and brokerage divisions opened my eyes to the possibilities within real estate for making positive impacts on those we served and the community. Far from the number-centric industry I had imagined, real estate was first and foremost a people business, all about building relationships and exceeding expectations.

The day my father led a blind man on a tour of a building was the day this truth fully altered my perception.

Our prospect, the Executive Director of the Federation for the Blind, was searching for a new headquarters and training facility. He thought Baltimore would be perfect. When he arrived wearing dark sunglasses and holding a long, walking stick, I looked to my father, speechless. But if my father was taken aback, he showed no signs of it. Quite naturally and comfortably, he inquired as to what information was most important and relevant for the director to garner from the tours. He listened, learned, and then at each building, my father would describe the layouts and amenities, which directions the windows faced, and other features of the buildings. Because I went into the tour with preconceived ideas—that only a person with sight could effectively judge and take in one building over another—I was limited and stymied in my ability to lead this man from prospect to tenant. My naivete assumed I needed to have a plan and to know all the answers in order to impress the client, but what this man revealed was that he had a much better idea for what the Federation and those that would be learning skills there needed than what I thought they might need.

All we had to do was ask good questions, listen, and support him.

The director used his long cane to navigate and judge the exteriors and interiors of the buildings. On the outside, he would feel for steps and cracks, the width of walkways, feet from the curb to the door. Inside, he would rub his hands along walls to identify the finish—brick or plaster—and measure the distance between windows. At the last building we showed him, he asked how it could accommodate loading for materials that would need to be delivered for the work being performed by the blind students. My father walked him to the loading door, and the gentleman placed his cane on the ground, raised it back up, and pronounced it, "Perfect! Four feet." Wanting to take in the clear height from the eaves to the floor, he again raised his cane and brought it back to the floor. "Twelve feet," he turned to my father, "this building could work."

I learned the power of possibilities that day, the value of listening first to others, seeing beyond what is in front of you, and always letting their words guide the strategies and decisions one makes as a leader.

Listening to and empowering others was at the heart of what teaching was all about too. Seeing the connections between the skill sets needed for the classroom and the skill sets needed for real estate fascinated me. At Manekin Corporation, I could be helping businesses find homes, helping them succeed, having them see us as stakeholders in their success, and helping them contribute to the community. Whatever technical skills I lacked,

I could learn. Wherever I fell short, I could fall back on Manekin's experienced team. What mattered most was believing real estate could be more than just bricks and sticks. I needed to believe going beyond the traditional role of landlord and tenant meant creating real and fundamental human connections and value.

In 1975, I entered the world of real estate.

# Section One

*Creating a Purposeful Company*

# 1. Start with a Higher Purpose

Imagine you're at the symphony. The conductor steps onto the rostrum and lifts the baton. Silence. Expectation. Then, magic. With a flick of the wrist, the conductor leads the orchestra through the music. But you barely notice them. Their silent guidance brings the violins to the forefront with a solo. Then they interweave the cellos, trumpets, and percussion with just a nod of the head or a swoop of the arm; the music continues and advances at just the right time. Musicians play with passion, their individual parts creating a glorious whole. Then the music crescendos, each instrument lifts its voice, and with a grand flourish, the finale leaves you breathless.

## Leaders as Orchestra Conductors

The strength of a leader is the same as the strength of a conductor— they know how to bring out the best in their people. Orchestra conductors intuitively know how the music should sound and are keenly aware of the experience they want the audience to have; similarly, leaders possess a bird's eye view of their organization's vision and understand how everyone con- tributes to the whole. Just like in an orchestra, every musician (or employee) is absolutely essential. A symphony is not a symphony if we hear only solos. The glory of a symphony—the success of it—depends upon each musician playing their part with passion, ecstatic to be part of the magic.

Consider the Humble Viola.

The violist has very few notes in the grand scheme of a symphony. She always takes a back seat, always offers support, rarely sees a solo. She waits through pages of rests before being called upon to passionately play maybe two lines. The audience barely distinguishes her section from the violins; indeed, many don't even realize her instrument exists! But the conductor knows how essential she is, and he's made sure she knows it too. Our Humble Viola revels in her part and how it fits with those around her. The conductor has made it clear how important her part is by giving her his enthusiastic support and full attention when it is time to lift her notes in harmony with the others; he does this for everyone, which means each musician feels his or her own worth and the worth of the others. The violist knows intimately the satisfaction that comes from being part of something larger than herself. Making music with others is the most sublime experience of her life—even if it means hours of practicing scales, even if it means the violins get all the melodies—that's not the point for her. The point is always this: creating something beautiful with others is meaningful beyond belief.

## Meaningful Beyond Belief Begins with a Higher Purpose

For my first four years with Manekin Corporation, I traveled back and forth between Baltimore and Columbia, conducting business. The work energized me, but the long commute each way was certainly not the best use of my time, especially when I might drive back and forth more than once a day. But in 1979, the company opened a satellite office in Columbia and offered me the opportunity to be its first intrapreneur within the larger company. I jumped at the chance. The incredible and inspiring vision and actions of a man named Jim Rouse, the developer responsible for envisioning the city of Columbia, between Baltimore and Washington, was key in the company's mind.

In the mid-sixties, the Rouse Company, under the leadership of its founder Jim Rouse, had the foresight to recognize the potential of the Baltimore Washington Corridor and Howard County's central position within this area. Jim knew that it was just a matter of time before developers would be eager to purchase parcels of land to start building—a strip mall here, an apartment and office complex there. And before you know it a city would be built with little or no foresight. But that didn't happen, because of Jim's vision. He was somehow able to quietly and without fanfare acquire

14,000 acres of land. Jim said to the Howard County leaders: You have a chance here to take control. Urbanization is inevitable in this corridor between two of the East Coast's most vital cities. If you start now with us, you get to plan for and exercise control over how your city grows. Jim's public relations campaign successfully convinced the leaders of rural Howard County and their electorate. "What do you want? What do you need?" he asked them. And then he built it for them. Rouse pulled people together with land planners and architects in community meetings and brought in future residents and businesses to weigh in and plan the outcomes.

Their city became Columbia, and it was built around the concept of village centers. People didn't just need homes; they needed accessible and quality healthcare, education, and retail. The twelve village centers were all connected so that children could leave their homes and walk through wooded paths to get to school, skirting traffic and maintaining both a sense of personal autonomy and connection to their neighbors. Rouse built it, and people came. They came not just because of its proximity to Baltimore and Washington or its easy access to three international airports and the Port of Baltimore, but because it was designed around the needs and input of those that would live, work, and play there. Rouse's approach to development was a new way to envision and design communities. He saw what no one else did because he listened to what everyone was saying. He listened to their wildest dreams and their worst fears; he made them stakeholders in the process, and in return, they gave him an abundance of insights and ideas. He took their ideas, shook them together, and created something that exceeded everyone's expectations. A city was born.

In the early days, I didn't even have an office — just a Volkswagen convertible and pocket full of dimes (for the payphones, of course). We started to build our team and lay our foundation for a genuine and purposeful company. Real estate shouldn't be just about leasing space; for us, it was about creating homes where companies felt like stakeholders in the process. People first. Function plus connection. Caring, thoughtful, engaged — acting from the inside-out.

We considered ourselves early pioneers in Columbia. We went into the market with notepads and pens, and just like Rouse, we listened. Countless listening sessions later, we'd design building configurations. The companies we selected as listening platforms were currently leasing small units tucked into corners of larger buildings where office space was cramped, adjacent to loading doors, and the only natural light came from the front doors. What if you were given a clean slate? We asked them. They said, offices, labs, and R&D space, plenty of natural lighting, functional and separate storage space. They gave us their ideal, their ideal gave them room to grow and we provided the space where that growth and success could happen. My classroom lessons were always coming back to me-growth happens when we meet people where they are, give them the resources and setting they need to thrive, and help them see what's possible. Our role is to give our full attention, observe and listen to them, so we can connect with them where they are and, after, develop strategies to implement change that supports them.

Developing single-story flex spaces was where we broke ground; we'd go on to build a lot more over the years, and this million-plus square foot portfolio continued to be a success. More than one-third of our original tenants grew over the years and continued to choose to work with us. They became more than tenants; they were family.

As I said, the Columbia branch was an opportunity for me to consciously engineer a new company from the ground up. The lessons from Jim Rouse were cornerstones on which to build. And we would need a new structure as well. That was developed by a man named Ray Blank.

Our company in Baltimore was successful, but it was not cohesive or integrated in the way I imagined our Columbia office could be. Baltimore functioned like a collection of superbly talented musicians—but all playing solos. Drawing inspiration from the orchestra director analogy, if I wanted this new company to perform as a symphony, then we'd need to emphasize team accomplishments, collaboration, and contribution to the whole. It would need to be different from how things had been done, and I knew it could work.

I called upon my mentor—our company's management consultant—Ray Blank, and he came up with a model so obvious I couldn't believe we hadn't been functioning this way already.

The basis for the model was this: To foster real motivation and direction, we needed to first define a higher purpose—a purposeful one. With a well-defined and meaningful vision, those joining the company could see, feel, and know exactly how their individual and collective efforts contributed to the whole. They could take ownership of the vision because they were clear in their roles and motivated within the company.

My vision and higher purpose for the Columbia branch of Manekin Corporation was to be visible and responsive partners and stakeholders in the success of those we developed for and for Howard County (where Columbia is located). When I was commuting more than once a day back and forth between Baltimore and Columbia, there was no way to be fully responsive to the companies we were building space for, or to the people who managed the buildings, or to the county we were developing in. We needed to have an established presence, so we could be seen as stakeholders in the success of those we developed for and in Howard County, and this not just in terms of economic development but in the quality of life too. Having a physical presence allowed us to be seen as neighbors and not as guests. It demonstrated that our day-to-day activities were genuine and focused on our higher purpose.

No matter where you happen to be in your leadership journey, it is important to take a step back and reflect on what the higher purpose for your company and its business endeavors are. By defining your purpose, you take the first giant step toward building a purposeful company that can leave a mark on the world for generations to come.

I offer you the idea of determining your purpose for the work you are doing or will be doing. Does it resonate inside of you and in those who work with you?

## Defining Your Purpose

You may or may not be at the beginning of starting your business. But if you are reading this, you may be at a crossroad of sorts or have some opportunity to transform how you move forward as a leader. To those just starting out, I'd like to address a common, and natural question, that I have often been asked from those at the beginning of their venture:

"So how do I get started? How do I take the leap?"

My answer to that isn't prescriptive. Each venture and every situation are unique, and building or rebuilding your career is a highly personalized endeavor. One that each must navigate according to their own interests, needs, abilities, and personalities. However, just like an orchestra conductor believes in the power of music and musicians to transform the symphony and touch the hearts of those who listen, so I ask you too: what do you believe in so deeply, so profoundly, that you are compelled to take a risk and start your enterprise or take your department to a new level? There is a piece in you that is full of purpose and extraordinary potential-something that stirs you up and personally affects you.

And that piece resides in your unique purpose.

Every great company is built on the purpose of its leader, and that becomes the guiding force to determine how to bring a meaningful product or service to the market. Your purpose has the power to change trajectories because it can reveal what is missing in the market and how to fill the gap. Your purpose is what people will resonate with. It is the passion and personality behind your entire company or department.

A purpose creates more than just an exchange between your company and the client; it creates a partnering and a belonging.

You might start to understand that it will matter little what you do if you don't know your purpose for doing it. Leadership guru and professor at Columbia University, Simon Sinek, describes how leaders stir action in his TED Talk, "How Great Leaders Inspire Action." He asks: What was it that Steve Jobs and the Apple team created that has customers waiting outside of Apple stores for hours, just to be the first to buy their new products, when there are so many other tech stores? Why did 250,000 people show up in Washington, DC in August of 1963 to hear Martin Luther King Jr.'s "I Have A Dream" speech when there were many other awe-inspiring civil rights activists also speaking up and out? Why did the Wright brothers, two gentlemen from Dayton, Ohio, with no college degree or capital, launch the first man-controlled plane and receive worldwide recognition for it when others were exploring and developing flight at the same time? The answer, according to Sinek, doesn't require an advanced degree. Each of those people had a higher purpose for the work they were doing. They truly believed they were creating a movement and making a difference.

When I had the opportunity to lead entrepreneurial classes at Loyola University, the MBA students' first assignment, before ever stepping into the classroom, was to watch that TED Talk by Sinek. From the beginning, I wanted them to resonate with Sinek's major theme that we must not seek the *what* in the work we do, but rather, in his words, "the *why*" or the purpose. Their semester-long project was to develop an entrepreneurial enterprise and was to be based on the premise that people buy products and services for their higher *purpose* not their *what*. Because of that, we must always consider questions like: Is there a higher purpose? Why is it meaningful? Will those buying from us do so because they feel it, relate to it, and believe in it?

To highlight just how specific you can get with your purpose and also how diverse purposes can be, I offer some real-life examples from: two student projects, two Baltimore organizations, and two professionals and entrepreneurs who team-taught with me at Loyola.

First, let's consider two of these student projects and how each one harnessed a higher purpose to bring meaning to their product and service so that it became more than producing something simply for the sake of consumption.

The first example is a student who began her presentation by showing a slide of a bloodied and battered woman—a woman who'd been accosted while out on a run. "As an early morning urban runner myself," she began, "I believe no person should feel unsafe pursuing a healthy and happy life." She wanted to develop a high-tech wristband that, when triggered, lets out a loud screeching sound and sends a signal to the police and to personal contacts, letting them know the user is in danger. Her device would be meaningful to the market and would fill a gap by reducing vulnerability and fear, thereby increasing feelings of safety, confidence, and peace.

Our second example is a student who worked in research that focused on children with rare diseases. Her experience gave her insight into the issues experienced by patients, physicians, and researchers dealing with rare chronic diseases, particularly how confused, isolated, and scared patients and families are when first diagnosed. The student wanted to start a non-profit organization with a unique case management model to provide the best coordinated care possible.

Our next two examples are Baltimore organizations founded by women. The students at Loyola and I ventured outside the classroom to visit these women and learn about their own important purposes.

Jennifer Green, a former urban teacher and administrator, had witnessed teachers burning out quickly and leaving the profession because they were not properly trained and supported. From this experience, she birthed Urban Teachers with this purpose: to provide opportunities for aspiring teachers to succeed in the classroom and achieve long-term tenure. She believed that in order to empower children through learning and to deliver equitable education, teachers needed to be empowered and supported first. Her organization set these teachers up to be surrounded by stakeholders— those that could provide guidance, insights, and direction to ensure their success. As a result, teachers were fully prepared to lead their classrooms and positively affect student outcomes.

Next, we visited with Jess Gardner, who founded Allovue. Jess had spent years in the urban classroom as a teacher and witnessed principals struggling to appropriate their school budgets with little support from the central office. Her purpose was to empower principals and help them feel like the CEOs of their schools. To do so, she created an app for principals to make it easy to take control of their school budgets.

Then there were the two seasoned professionals who came to the classroom to teach alongside me. They shared a powerful common purpose in their commitment to serving others.

George Mister, the accountant for Seawall, sees himself as so much more than someone who just does year-end taxes. He believes in helping entrepreneurs succeed by empowering them with knowledge—knowledge that will affect their business every day. He guides them in understanding and utilizing their balance sheets as a tool, so they know how their business is actually performing.

Don Zeithaml, one of our attorneys, believes he offers more than advice to new companies setting up their legal entity. He believes in digging in deep with his clients and understanding where they see their company in the future, so he can help them set a strong foundation now. His forward thinking and deep knowledge help entrepreneurs establish the right legal structures now to support their company's growth in the best way later.

Whether or not the Loyola students developed and launched their purpose into actual entrepreneurial ventures was not the goal. It was for each of them to have the opportunity to see themselves thinking and acting in a larger context. The point was to see more clearly how they could take the off-site visits and knowledge from the presenters and apply it to their own projects, and just maybe to their everyday journeys. Students moved from the classroom experience to real time. They were able to hear from leaders how they had moved their purposes to become actual organizations and consider how they too could implement this into their own entrepreneurial enterprises.

The student whose project was to create a hi-tech wristband wrote in her final evaluation that she took a lot of time reading articles, talking to fellow runners, and understanding the need for the product/technology. She even set up a mock investor presentation and convinced five of her coworkers to sit in as she presented, so she could practice and so they could give her real time, honest feedback.

When Thibault came to me looking to start a real estate company, he had a very strong purpose. He wanted us to be identified not as real estate developers but as a group of social entrepreneurs who would use the built environment to empower communities, unite cities, and help launch powerful ideas. To that end, we would help build communities where those occupying the buildings, and those living in and around them, would be empowered to engage with and set the direction of the developments. Thibault wanted real estate to make a difference and provide real value for those it served. As we took steps to pursue this higher purpose, it evolved in specificity. We believed, and started to see in new ways, that teachers and nonprofit organizations that support public education and communities are doing the most important economic development work in the city. It is through them that the next generation of leaders are created. The leaders who will help once again make disinvested communities great places to live, work, and play. Therefore, we built Seawall upon the higher purpose of engaging everyone who would be affected by our developments as stakeholders in the process, empowering them to have a say in every decision.

From an inside-out perspective, every purpose must have its own soul if it is to be effective. What is your purpose? How do you see it filling a gap in the market and being transformative? Define your purpose and then direct it toward everything you do. It is your passion, your philosophy, your drive, your gift of insight to be used in service to others. When your purpose is put into service for other people, you can be confident that it will reach new heights.

I have seen this approach to purpose and inside-out leadership grow by staying in touch with Loyola students over the years. One of the graduate students, Brad Viers, who now works for a large company, shared his insights into one's higher purpose: "If a purpose is grounded in just having enough money, food, gadgets, vacations, well—eventually those needs will probably get met. What then? Ultimately, our needs run out of the need to be satisfied. Yet there will always be more to do, more to give, more to provide, serve, and share within our communities. Ground your reason for being in a service-based mentality and you'll find you have a lifetime supply of motivation to propel you forward."

Now that you are thinking about a higher purpose to fuel your company and connect your team, let's take a look at how a relationship-oriented business model can help you build your company.

# 2. Keep it Simple

An inside-out leader knows he or she is not the "head of the pack." They know they are not equipped with all the knowledge and influence needed to, guide their people through any obstacle and on to glory alone. They know as leaders that they do not possess all the answers, and they don't have to be everywhere and do everything. These understandings incorporate the most important aspect of good business: the power of the people.

Good leaders know they don't need to know it all and do it all. They lean on the wisdom and seek the guidance of their entire team, their stakeholders, their clients, and the communities they serve. These leaders, though, do require a relationship-oriented model to bring their company or team together as a collective whole.

Only then will business leaders truly know what the conductor knows: Even though the purpose of a symphony is to produce beautiful music—the conductor never makes a sound.

Benjamin Zander, the current musical director for the Boston Philharmonic Orchestra and the Boston Philharmonic Children's Orchestra, said it emphatically in his powerful presentation at the 2011 European Zeitgeist called "Choosing Your World":

> The conductor depends, for his power, on his ability to make the musicians powerful. In their minds and hearts, they know what the music should sound like and what the audience should feel as they sit and take it in. The conductor has a vision, and they bring this out by empowering every one of the musicians.

A great leader connects employees to their intrinsic purpose and then steps back and lets them shine. But how to do this strategically, without being everywhere at once and knowing everything? When leaders empower others, they turn others into leaders—who then empower others.

## An Inside-Out Approach

When I first came on board at Manekin Corporation in the '70s, I learned that the company's ultimate goal had been Total Tenant Satisfaction. Between our six departments—development, construction, brokerage, property management, investment sales, and administration—we had great intentions and superb talent. And yet, the right hand often didn't know what the left was doing. Deadlines weren't met, good communication was lacking, and as a result, occupancy dates were not always realized. This left nobody, not the least of all the end users, satisfied.

I asked myself, what could we do better?

As I knew Columbia was going to be my new home and that we would be building a satellite office over time, I'd been picking up a lot of business books, trying to get ideas for a new approach. The messages tended to be the same: An inefficient work environment and weakly inspired company culture stem from a faulty set of beliefs that transcend surface-level issues like departmental communication or new hire orientation. That's a lot of fancy jargon to say that our issues with disconnect came from the foundational structure of the company. Where there was disconnect, I wanted to bring cohesion. Where I struggled to set direction and help those that would be working with us find purpose in their work, I hoped to bring clarity and motivation. Seeing the need for improvement is one thing and knowing how to get there is another. So now what?

Ray Blank, one of the most curious and bohemian of souls I had ever met, once again came to my assistance. As I shared earlier, Ray was the company's management consultant, and he was also my mentor and a friend. He was, hands down, a crucial piece of our company's success, a true force of nature, and one who was intensely plugged into effective organizational dynamics and the human experience within a company. (Let me take this moment to say—surround yourself with smart people who want to work with you and teach you. People who are invested in your success as a leader.) After describing my dilemma to Ray, he stood up abruptly from the table, grabbed his jacket, and said, "I need a walk." I smiled and waited. I'd grown accustomed to his curious need to "think on his feet." Thirty minutes later, Ray sat down in front of me and said, "I've got it."

He started out by recognizing that the overall company had six departments, each seemingly functioning as its own company. Ray saw that synergy was needed in the process of conceiving, overseeing, and completing projects. What we needed was to use the collective wisdom of both internal and external teams to plan, deliver, and maintain what was best for the businesses in Columbia that called our buildings home. He shared that what we needed was to play like a symphony, and he had more than a few ideas.

First, the philosophical: The new model wants to emphasize purpose over tasks. (This is what I discussed in the previous chapter.) There needs to be a higher purpose for the work being done, one that is intentional and well-designed, so that each person and the team members understand how their individual and collective efforts make a difference to the tenants, the building, the company, and the community.

Next, the active—or the how: This portion needs to communicate the methods by which responsibilities are to be delivered. The methods were to be grounded in cohesive, organized, and thoughtful teams that focused their efforts on service to others—having great relationships with contractors and seeing them as partners, not vendors, celebrating the work done as teams, and believing that as we worked more effectively and efficiently as a team, we could maximize client satisfaction.

Finally, the functional—the what: The leader of the team needs to be able to develop responsibilities with each team member as to their individual and collective roles.

Ray then stood up and went to the easel, picked up the marker, and drew two circles. He shared that this inside circle was to be the purpose of the team that will be built. It houses the companies we build for, the buildings we develop, and the larger community we serve. The outside circle would be those responsible to serve the companies, develop and maintain the projects, and serve the larger community. Although each person has a function, they see themselves fully interconnected, focusing on what's in the center of the circle. Each team would be like its own company. They will be fully responsible and accountable to develop, finance, construct, market, maintain, and administer each project that they develop.

## Bringing Inside-Out to Life

This approach, different from what was in place when I entered the company, gave full responsibility to the team and empowered the members to see each other as equals rowing in the same direction.

Looking at the easel with the inside-out model, I asked myself, could it really be this simple? Yes. It could.

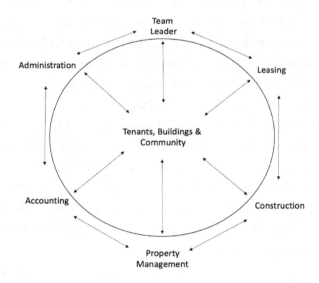

After forty-plus years of implementing this inside-out model (not only in real estate but in education and the nonprofit sector as well), I can tell you with confidence—it really is this straightforward. It isn't a magic bullet for success, yet it is truly transformational. Beyond that, it is just so fulfilling. This methodology and structure have the key elements needed to foster real motivation and direction, making it possible for those working together to feel clear and motivated in their roles within the company. When that happens, it breeds a sense of ownership, self-assigned and team direction, and larger purpose. And when that happens, then you can finally reach total satisfaction and more—awakening possibilities in the client's needs and dreams and far exceeding all their expectations.

As Simon Sinek says: "When people inside the company know why they come to work, people outside the company are vastly more likely to understand why the company is special. In these organizations, from the management on down, no one sees themselves as any more or any less than anyone else. They all need each other. They work for a purpose."

The essence of the model is to show teams and their members who they are serving and how, when working together, the whole would be greater than the sum of its parts, enabling them to exceed expectations.

Here is an example of the property managers at Seawall, years down the road, using the same inside-out model that Ray developed during that meeting back in the '70s.

PURPOSE:

As the property manager, I will have the incredible opportunity to create long-term value by providing services that exceed expectations and where the environment is one that makes the project a once-in-a-lifetime experience for those working in, living in, and surrounding our developments. Through my day-to-day activities, and those on our team and others at Seawall, the building will operate efficiently, effectively, and in a manner that will maximize tenant satisfaction, return on investment (human and financial), and make a significant contribution to the neighborhoods that surround the project.

METHOD:

We will carry out our efforts as a cohesive team working for the common goal of exceeding expectations. We will be thoughtful and organized in how our efforts are actually performed, understanding that all our efforts are for those we serve. We will work with the companies that provide services not as vendors but as partners.

FUNCTION:

I will develop and execute programs with the team that ensure the building is exceptionally well maintained, tenant satisfaction is high, and the office is properly managed in a fashion that allows those working together to feel responsible for the company's success.

## Empowered People Empower People

Our inside-out approach to building a genuine company through a relationship-oriented business model didn't stop with our core team. We imbued it into every project, every meeting, every interaction. This model was the basis for teams to feel free to get creative in their approaches. A simple example would be cold-calling. At the time (and still today), many real estate companies focused on cold calling to find clients and drum up business. We didn't do this. We built relationships with real estate brokers, and then these brokers—who had relationships with clients looking for space for their companies—brought clients to us. This created more organic, intentional, and personalized experiences from the outset. This didn't surprise us because it very much fit with what we believed about the power of relationships.

What did surprise us, however, was that this would also be something that attracted some of our best employees to us. One of our early hires described it thus:

> In my previous real estate office, the hierarchy was apparent and quite militaristic. I was aware of my place in the world, and that place was definitely at the bottom. My boss sent me out every day to knock on doors and cold-call; he told me not to come back until I had four cards. "You get 'em in the door, and I'll take it from there," he'd say, believing my youth and attractiveness were his secret weapons to get clients. While I can say the experience was . . . character building, it was also demoralizing. I'd get my quota of business cards and then go sit in the mall the rest of the day, dreading going back to that office environment. I was relieved and

amazed when Manekin Corporation said to me, "No, we don't cold-call. We have a wonderful list of brokers, and if they know us and our projects because we market to them, then they can put together a client and developer." It was night-and-day different getting hired at Manekin. They valued me. There was a level of respect that was incredibly different from what I was used to. All relationships were valued, whether client, contractor, or vendor. And if you have that relationship, everything else can work out. I felt so nurtured and supported by the company and the leaders that it made it so easy for me to go out and find ways to invest in our brokers, prospects, and tenants in ways that would really make them feel just as special and important too.

Now feeling empowered and valued in a company, she was free to act instinctively—and her instincts knew that building relationships was what it was all about, and this was something she could do flawlessly. After her initial meeting with a prospect, her role was to develop a relationship with them as their company became one of our tenants. We would send customer satisfaction surveys out after new companies moved into our spaces, and time and time again, they referenced her as having exceeded all their expectations, praising how she helped them execute all aspects of their relocation seamlessly.

## Strategies and Methods for a Relationship Model

## A Little Thing Called 5-15s

As I mentioned earlier, as a leader, you cannot be everywhere at once. Maybe in the beginning, when you have just a couple of employees, but as your company grows, you will find it is imperative that you take intentional steps to stay connected to the pulse of those working with you. Ray Blank helped me find a way to do this through a simple concept he called "5-15" reports. These reports served an obvious function by creating a system for each team member to reflect on their week and check in with their manager. It kept leadership connected to those working with them, and therefore, connected to the higher purpose. And they also serve a deeper, less obvious function.

The heart and soul of 5-15 reports are to celebrate what has been accomplished and to brainstorm together ways to get missed tasks back on track.

Here's how it works. Every Friday, each employee writes a fifteen-minute mind dump of their week. They explain why, in their minds, their efforts worked, and if they didn't work, what caused them to fall short. They write it in whatever format they like: handwritten, typed, in bullet points. Then, over the weekend, the team leader would give themselves five minutes or so to read over each report. Simple, but it prepared them to enter the new work week ready for an intentional and thoughtful face-to-face meeting with each person on the team.

As crucial and helpful as these obviously were to team leaders and other managers, they also were very helpful to those who wrote them. From the employee perspective, it allowed them to review their week with a critical eye, see their accomplishments, focus on what they needed to get done and ALWAYS feel heard and important. It created connection.

Keeping in touch with the pulse of those working with you is an important piece to implementing a relationship-oriented model. That's why taking the time to actually meet in person and respond verbally, not through emails, is quite crucial. An important part of a leader's role is to not only communicate the company's vision, but also to demonstrate it, by making the time to meet person to person.

Great leaders help others know why they get out of bed each morning, and that starts with leaders showing others that they themselves care, are present, and are listening.

## Bi-Monthly Performance Criteria

Another strategy we used to communicate the methods of responsibilities and to stay connected to our teams was to implement bi-monthly performance criteria meetings. In many companies, performance criteria reviews are typically done once a year, and that makes it hard to stay on top of ever-changing goals and objectives. One might come into their yearly review meeting and say, "Well, here's what happened last year. So next year, I think I'd like to meet with more real estate brokers." What individuals want to pursue in their work needs to be measurable and attainable if they're going to be successful. Meeting once a year keeps goals too broad, distant, and incalculable. Since performance review meetings are so valuable, it seems unfortunate to contain them to just the end of the year. By upping the frequency of these meetings, everyone in the company is pushed to be more intentional and thoughtful about goals and how to accomplish them.

Here's how we did it. When new people came on board, criteria was immediately established together. Both parties knew and agreed upon the expectations. We offered them an idea of the purpose, method, and function of their position to give them scope of the job and to support their success, and we also asked for their input and feedback about the position and how they saw their own purpose, their how, and their what being played out. We asked questions like, "What can you think about that could make the job more meaningful for you and impact your efforts with clients, vendors, and those working with you?" Since they were the ones doing the job and holding themselves accountable, it was important to follow their lead on the goals and aspirations they had for the role. Then we rated each task on a scale of 1 – 10, with 6 – 10 being what was to get accomplished first before tackling the smaller tasks if there was time left over.

Those criteria were then reviewed every six weeks or so to see what was accomplished, and to plan for the next six weeks. The wonderful thing was our office in Columbia was small, the team leaders and I were not behind our desks. We were able to be an integral part of the team's success by being with them out in the field and helping them do the work they wanted to accomplish. When we'd sit together, side by side, reviewing the list, I'd ask, "OK, so this task was a ten. What was the performance?" And they were honest. If it was only a nine out of ten, we marked it as such. And we discussed how it was accomplished. For those responsible for leasing for example, we'd discuss things such as; "how many brokers can you see during these next six weeks?" The number would always be achievable. And we'd settle on deadlines—should some of these projects get accomplished in the third or in the fourth week? And what I loved best was the time we had to simply brainstorm together about the work, about what might be standing in the way, and what tools were needed to help goals get accomplished. It was useful for them and for me.

At the end of the year, when we did salary reviews, we didn't even need to do an end-of-year review because we'd been doing the work all along, every month or so with each individual. We knew, instinctually, what every person was doing and what was going on in every facet of the company.

Whether doing weekly, monthly, or yearly meetings, whether planned or unplanned, time spent with those working with you should never be measured by the clock. Sitting next to your employees creates a more personal connection. Comfortable sofas in the conference room or office foster an atmosphere that invites trust and togetherness. Sit back, listen to each other's thoughts, exchange ideas, and let time unfold. What you discover might just be extraordinary. Leaders can and must always be thinking of ways, big and small, to create meaningful moments and positive interactions with everyone they work with.

# 3. Align Others with the Vision

An orchestra conductor knows how to interpret the music, understands how all the parts and pieces fit together, and then empowers the musicians to play together. As leaders, we must know how to interpret the vision of the company to our staff, surround ourselves with people who align with that vision, and then empower them in their roles to take responsibility and to act creatively. This requires the ability to get to the core of a person's values and to find out what makes them tick. Look for strengths—for passion—and invest in those. This is an ever-going process that requires inside-out leadership.

When people have come to work with us, they don't really believe they're in the real estate business. They believe they're in the business of building community and using real estate as the means to that end. And that's exactly what they should believe. That's the vision that we've built. Whether you're a potential resident or the person bussing the leftovers after a guest's amazing meal, whether you're the architect designing the building or the electrician wiring it, you're an ambassador of the purpose behind the company. It's the job of a leader to make sure others understand how significant they really are.

Leadership is foremost about building relationships, not transactions. While it's easy to understand and accept this idea as it relates to customers and end users, authentic relationships are truly at the core of every great company—from managing those that work with you right down to hiring new ones. The art is to align your team with your vision.

Building your symphony of passionate players can begin on day one of the interview process.

## Beyond the Resume: Hiring for Value

Since genuine leaders know that each employee must feel their role is significant to the success of the company, the leader's job then is to help them align with the company's vision and experience themselves as stakeholders within it—and that begins with the hiring process. You might think that, as a successful real estate company, we hired people with a background in real estate, but you'd be surprised at how often that was not the case. We hired people for their values, and that's not something you can always discover just from a resume.

A resume is a sterile thing. It tells why a person should be hired, and it reveals nothing about their soul—how they think, the words they use, or what they feel. If you go into the hiring process with a list of questions, you're going to come out with a list of answers. It's far too rote and, I've found, it's mostly unnecessary. When we hire someone, we don't just want to know if the person will be a good fit or if they have the credentials to do the job. We want to know: will they be happy in their endeavors? Will they be fulfilled as a person in this position? A good leader knows the power of hiring employees who find joy and meaning in their work, and more importantly, a good leader nurtures and honors that.

Part of helping others align with your vision is often quite simply finding those who already resonate with it.

Finding the right people for your company is an art, not a science. In an interview, I'm moving beyond cerebral decision-making, and I am trusting my gut. I'm reading body language, and I'm looking for that buoyancy of voice, that sparkle in the eyes that tells me the person can really imagine themselves at our company, and indeed, already is imagining it.

## Going with Your Gut

David showed up to our interview in Columbia as one might expect— with a firm handshake and wearing a blazer and slacks, crisp shirt, and smart tie. It was a gorgeous, early spring day, and he did everything "right"-neat resume, neat clothes, etc. I wasn't looking for how well he conformed to professional standards of presenting oneself to prove success. I was looking for soul, and that's not something you can wrap up in a resume or a suit. Our office was small; calling it a closet wouldn't be too far from the truth. The point is, there was nowhere to hold a private conversation, so I suggested we head outdoors for a stroll. First, I took David's jacket from him, hanging the formality of what it represented on a hook.

"You were one of the first people to respond to our ad in the paper about this position. We're small but we have significant opportunities, and while it's important we hire someone able to turn prospects into tenants, it's even more important we hire someone who gets our vision."

"Well, as I said in my resume, I was the assistant vice president at—"

Not to offend David, I pleasantly stopped him there and said, "I know what your resume says, and it's impressive! And to be honest, I don't want to talk about why you *could* do this job. I'd like to know what excited you about your old job, and if nothing did—what excites you about this one?"

"OK . . . yeah! Well, that's easy-community building. Sales is about so much more than closing a deal. I haven't worked in real estate before, but what excites me about this position is that when we're helping someone find a home for their business, we're actually helping connect the community-change it. And hopefully, we leave it better than we found it."

I loved that he used "we" so liberally. Whether a person speaks in first-person singular or first-person plural offers a good hint into how they really think. Is everything all about them? Or is everything all about the company and the customers? It's not just in business, though. How does your interviewee talk about family? "I planned and took my family on this great vacation," or "We took this great trip!" It's a subtle difference, and I've found the people who are the best fit for our company have been we-oriented and relationship-minded.

I urged David on. "Tell me more about the community you live in. What do your daughters do for fun after school?"

When I interview people, I want to know what's happening in their world—what they're up to. I learn so much more about their personality this way. David's hands came out of his pockets, his gestures got big, and his enthusiasm was clear. He didn't just want a job to do; he wanted a job to get behind and pour himself into. We had just circled back to the front of the office building and sat down on the curb when one of the principals in the company rolled up in his car. He had been out with some lenders and had a six-pack of beer left over from that meeting. "Want one?" he asked, putting the cans in our hands. "Cheers!"

The beer was warm, like the day, but good, like the feeling in my gut about David. He had all the right instincts about what his job would be about, and he was all about relationships.

"David," I said, "our space is small, but we sure would love to squeeze another desk in for you. We'd love to have you join us here at Manekin Corp. What do you say?" With a wide grin he said, "Yes!"

## Building on Strengths

One of the first steps toward implementing this new model of a purposeful company operating from the inside-out was to listen, observe, and empower. This was accomplished through intentionally long meetings (remember: get rid of the clock) that helped us move beyond qualifications and really get to know our employees' strengths and personalities while also helping them build a vision of themselves as stakeholders within the company.

When I hired David, it was on the strength of his communication skills. I didn't know anything about his organizational skills. That I learned as time went on. With each newly signed lease, David was to prepare a lease abstract with the salient points of the terms. This was critically important for those administering and accounting for the lease. I didn't think much about it until I learned that they were not getting done.

During one of our long one-on-one meetings, I brought it up. It turns out, it wasn't that David could not do the paperwork, but that it just wasn't a priority. His strengths laid elsewhere. From having gone out into the field with David, I learned something about him that I never would have picked up on otherwise. His way with people was second to none. Great at earning their trust, he moved them with perfect precision from suspect to prospect to tenant.

There happened to be a book I had read called *Now Discover Your Strengths* written by Marcus Buckingham and Donald Clifton, and one major premise of the book was that companies invest millions converting weaknesses to strengths when instead they should be investing those same dollars in taking strengths to new levels. David's style was different from how I had originally envisioned his position, yet it was in total alignment with everything the company believed in. His strengths were in building relationships.

During one of those long meetings, he showed me how he had mapped out a way to have more one-on-one interactions with people and it actually met our customers' needs much better than how our industry typically operates. Who was I to stand in his way? If I released him from his obligation to do paperwork, I freed him to do what he did best and to do it with more joy and ease.

Now, lease abstracts and other paperwork still had to get done—eventually—and I realized the best course of action was simply to hire someone else who enjoyed knowing the work they were doing was meaningful and also enjoyed being behind the scenes, with little desire to interact with prospects. We brought on Karen Dean, who was invigorated as an administrator and who excelled in that role. David and Karen would meet as needed so David could share with her the pertinent information the company needed to track. It was a win for everyone.

So, why not take natural skills and innate passions to a new level rather than worrying about converting weaknesses to strengths? A good leader is quick to say, "Why not? Let's try it! The worst that can happen is it fails." The change brought new energy and effectiveness into our company. David's communication style and actions inspired others working in Columbia. They saw that he was a stakeholder in the company; his ideas had been heard and his strategy trusted. It inspired them to find new ways to breathe life into their own projects and connect them to the greater mission—going above and beyond client expectations.

Leaders who wish to cultivate a purposeful company work to ensure that each employee knows their role is valuable and understands how it contributes to the whole. The leader interprets the company's vision for his or her team so well that they can't help but take ownership of and align with the vision too. As humans, we are hardwired to want to contribute to something bigger than ourselves, and the leader is the one who can see everything from 40,000 feet and show them how they are connected to and a key part of the grand plan. When people come to work feeling connected to a greater mission and knowing their work truly matters, they come in earlier, stay later, and go out of their way to connect with others about projects they are working on and how to bring them to life in the best way possible. This is the reality of realizing that joy, belonging, and satisfaction in one's work are better motivators than anything else I have found.

When we have those, we want to give beyond ourselves. It makes for a genuine company culture.

# Section Two

*Building Relationships*

# 4. Prioritize Relationships at Every Level

The highest long-term return on investment and human capital for any organization, for-profit or nonprofit, comes from one simple mindset: always work to exceed expectations. And before we are able to exceed those expectations, we have to cultivate a mindset and an atmosphere throughout our company where teams and those on the team feel empowered and motivated to give beyond their best. To exceed expectations, a genuine company must be grounded in team-driven and relationship-oriented models and philosophies. That's what this next section of chapters is about.

We've already discussed how to start with a higher purpose and align others with it, and then how to assemble a dynamic team. Now it is time to discuss bringing a human-centered and team-focused approach to your company by empowering those who work with you to take ownership of their role.

The success of any project depends on others feeling like stakeholders in the process, and that success depends on you, the leader, recognizing the efforts and talents around you. Building relationships, not transactions, has proven to be the firmest foundation upon which I could ever hope to build. The people in your company and the people in the field working with your company are co-creators and co-collaborators. They are the catalyst behind any great idea and behind all achievements. Learning how to create an environment that fosters empowerment, appreciation, and acknowledgment brings out the best in those who work with you. To create that environment, you have to first go inside yourself and nurture an authentic, deep-rooted appreciation for others that you then extend to everyone you meet, in both your personal and professional life.

It's a character trait that will never let you down.

## Deep-Rooted Appreciation

Inside-out leaders embody deep-rooted appreciation as a direct way to prioritize relationships over transactions. This appreciation is about celebrating those around us, taking ourselves (and our egos) out of the spotlight, and honoring the talents and efforts of those that work with us. Since relationships are at the center of your company, learning to prioritize them on every level is key to becoming an inside-out leader. There are so many ways, big and small, privately and publicly, to do this, and this mindset goes beyond just the company team. Deep-rooted appreciation is for all—the janitor and the Harvard grad, the folks pouring concrete and the folks poring over legal documents.

Because they carry such an appreciation for others, inside-out leaders also never believe that success is something they earned for themselves. Success is always about others.

We must always be thinking: How do we help others succeed, and when they do succeed, how do we honor them? It is our job as leaders to help those working with us, whether internally or externally, to know they are integral parts of the team, that they make a difference, and are critical to the project's success. It is especially important to remember to acknowledge and appreciate all the unsung heroes who come in day after day and do the tedious and grueling work necessary for a project's success with no thought of recognition, let alone glory.

As leaders, we bear witness to the talents and efforts of those working under our leadership and then let them know: "We're here because of you, and we wouldn't be here without you."

## Shining the Spotlight on Others

Remember the Miller's Court project mentioned in the introduction? Seawall's very first development turned a former manufacturing building into both residential units to house teachers new to Baltimore and collaborative office spaces for nonprofits that directly support education. We had engaged and collaborated with the entire community, and even so, when the day came to cut the ribbon and hand over keys to the new tenants, the huge audience turn-out exceeded all our expectations.

Thibault took to the stage as emcee to introduce the others who shared the platform with him: the governor, the mayor, the city council president, the school system CEO, department heads, and lenders. The people in the crowd included our commercial and residential tenants as well as the neighborhood associations, but they also included the contractors whose employees—the real heroes—were responsible for completely transforming this long-vacant structure into a beautiful building that would become a source of pride for the entire community. In hindsight, we should have provided seats in the front row for those that actually performed in the field—the electricians, plumbers, carpenters, and construction workers of all types—to show even greater appreciation for them.

When Thibault stood to speak, the story he shared was not about Seawall or the building; it was about everyone who made the development possible, including one woman in particular: the woman behind the counter at city government who processed all the construction drawings for the permits needed to renovate the Miller Building. "Karen," Thibault said, "was truly indispensable to seeing this project through to completion. Her job was crucial for the functioning of the office, yet her role is not one many are aware of." He continued to paint Karen as the ideal caring and professional civil servant, as knowledgeable and as helpful as they come, whose great disposition was such a joy and relief to us throughout the process as she was always available to answer our questions when we came to her office or phoned with questions and updates. From where I was sitting, I could see the mayor scribbling some notes during Thibault's speech-just adding to her upcoming remarks, I assumed.

A few days after the ceremony, when I found myself in the municipal office building where Karen worked, I learned the truth of those scribbles. "Donald!" Karen pulled me into a corner. "The mayor called me. *Directly.*"

She was beaming. "She told me what Thibault said at the ribbon-cutting ceremony and said she had wanted to call and congratulate me on my 'extraordinary efforts!'" I laughed with joy for her. "But Karen, this is wonderful and well-deserved!" "That's not all," she continued. "She's invited my husband and me to be her guests at a Ravens football game!" Her ear-to-ear smile said it all.

When we, as leaders, take the time to lift others up in the public eye, we directly empower their sense of value and worth in themselves and the community. This helps to solidify their esteem and enthusiasm to continue doing their best work possible. As humans, we are all wired to want to contribute to something bigger than ourselves. We want our efforts to be rewarded in ways that go beyond just monetary compensation for our time and talents. And so, this is what we, as leaders, must strive to provide for all our workers. Yes, a good salary is necessary and useful. And I do believe it's important to pay employees and contractors above industry standards as it shows direct care and concern; but, whereas money is a one-dimensional reward, esteem and purpose fulfill multiple aspects of our human needs.

Brad Viers, the MBA student from Loyola I spoke of earlier, shared with me that "as our modern world moves further from a world where survival and providing for self must be top of mind, employees are given freedom to make employment decisions based less on what physically provides the most, and more on what is emotionally, socially, and spiritually fulfilling. With this freedom, employees become less motivated to perform in exchange for physical needs being met (again, in no other time have there been so many options for individuals to satisfy basic needs); and therefore, employers are in a position of needing to motivate with a less tangible human need—a connection to a higher purpose." Inside-out leadership recognizes that honoring others helps them become their best, and connects them to a higher purpose, and when they are at their best then they find joy and satisfaction in bringing their best to you and the company.

So often, the public sees only one or two people at the top receiving fame and recognition for a job well done, but every masterpiece requires a team of people to bring it to life-a team of people with the work ethic and humility to show up, day after day, giving their all for the sake of something great. As the leader, it's probably going to be you up on that stage. You'll be the one to see all the smiles and receive all the words of thanks, which is precisely why you must be the one to step out of the spotlight and shine it on others. A purposeful company depends on the leader's ability to remove all ego and lead from a place of deep-rooted appreciation for others.

## Basking in the Reflected Glow

Ego: We all have it to some degree and how we use it defines us to those we work with and serve. Each of us can, even with our egos, learn to lead from a place of humility. We need simply to turn our attention to others, put ourselves in their shoes, and redefine success as: Where do we take pride and joy?

Inside-out leaders are most proud when they can sit back and bask in the reflected glow of the successes of their team. Their joy is similar to the orchestra conductor's—they get satisfaction from bringing their symphony together and empowering them to play their best and exceed the audience's expectations. When the music is beautiful, the conductor glows, knowing all along who was responsible. The music then is their reward, not the applause or the standing ovation. The orchestra conductor will always get recognition, though; this is just a reality. The newspapers will write about their flawless ear or their transcendent insight. So know that as a leader in your company, you will most likely be the person others will point to and recognize. In those moments, remember to speak about the people who really make the music happen. Let that be your source of pride, of joy, of satisfaction. It is a gift to be in a position to witness the people doing the jobs that never get sung because that means you are the one in the best position to praise them.

As soon as the accolades or the conversations are moving in a direction that elevate the company's accomplishment and your leadership, be sure to emphasize and cast the light on all the others who really made it happen. When you're with one of your associates and you happen to connect with someone who knows of your work, take the time to introduce them to the person who works with you. Give them all the accolades they deserve in front of this new audience. Highlight something that they have done or are doing that has exceeded expectations. When I'm with visitors at our projects and I see Enrique and Kevin, the men who maintain the buildings, I stop the group and introduce the men, saying it's because of their efforts the building always looks so great.

Appreciation, humility, basking in the reflected glow—perhaps all this sounds a bit too feel good, but all I can offer in reply is this: the proof is in the outcome. Some scientific research to back up these feel-good philosophies certainly lends credibility, though. The *Wall Street Journal* published a compelling article about humility in the workplace called "The Best Bosses Are Humble Bosses." In it, they discuss research that reveals how leading with humility allows us to keep improving ourselves, being aware of our weaknesses, and therefore, appreciative of what we can learn from listening to others. When compared to teams with less than humble bosses, the work from teams with humble leaders was of higher quality; and when senior executives led with humility, the entire company saw an increase in "efficiency, innovation, and profitability."

Efficiency, innovation, profitability-these are all good words and good company goals. But what the article states is closer to what I learned back teaching in the classroom: leadership is about providing learning opportunities in supportive settings. Success is met through collaboration. Like I've said before, being a great leader and a successful businessperson doesn't require an advanced degree, but it does require a love of people and empathy for others that enable one to lead from a place of deep-rooted appreciation, a place that allows them to make room for others and to listen and learn from them.

## Appreciation in Practice

Celebrating others is all about keeping your eyes open for ways to encourage those around you. Be ever on the lookout for new ways to show appreciation and to go above and beyond in support of those under our leadership.

One of the best ways to begin is to never underestimate the power of words. Simply taking the time to thank someone has tremendous power and can make all the difference in how that person feels about their work. At the end of every workday, when I grabbed my coat to head home, I walked through the office, and, to those that were still there, I'd say, in addition to a goodnight, a thank you. "Thank you for being here. Thank you for all you're doing and the time you put in every day. Thank you for helping make what we do so worthwhile."

There are countless ways to celebrate others; for example, I was also always on the move, never behind my desk if possible, bringing coffee and donuts to the crews out on the job sites early in the morning, and beer and pizza to the guys pulling an all-nighter to finish a project on time. Sending birthday, anniversary, or sympathy cards—these small gestures go a long way. When going on a job site or into a meeting and seeing a new face, the first thing I did was introduce myself. I do believe leaders ought to be on a first-name basis with everyone. Good leaders don't forget names. Bringing a human touch to our interactions—like holding the door open for the workers carrying ladders inside—and employing that human touch regularly helps foster real relationships, builds strong connections among teams of workers, and gives them the feeling they are valuable and what they do is important.

Showing appreciation is really very often about showing decency, and at times, it is about going beyond decency and actually putting yourself fully in the other person's shoes.

For example, Karen, who I mentioned earlier, was originally hired to support the marketing group and then later took the lead as the construction administrator. Karen loved to be behind the scenes doing the work that allowed those in the field to do what was most important-keeping our construction efforts moving forward. When, many years later, Karen was diagnosed with cancer and couldn't come in to work regularly, it was critical that we continue to pay her. She had looked out for our company all those years; we were going to look out for her. Sometimes, she needed to come into the office just to feel like her life was normal, just for a change of pace.

She couldn't do much when she was here, and that didn't matter. We paid her like we always paid her. Her job was hers until she passed away. We never wanted anyone to feel like they were replaceable. We wanted to be stakeholders in their health and success, just as they were stakeholders in the company's success.

Then there was the time one of our associates went into early, labor and her child was born with health issues that required months in the NICU. Having four children of my own, the turmoil she and her husband must have been experiencing was beyond my comprehensions-such a difficult time for a new family. The last thing I wanted was for her to worry about coming to work. The best thing was for her and her husband to be with their baby as often as possible. We insisted that she spend as much time every day with the baby as she needed. There was never an issue about her pay. It wasn't about the money. Because of our support, she was able to be a happier mom and bring that joy with her when she returned to work. Her success is another example of what happens when a company prioritizes relationships and recognizes the value of all those working in the organization.

Another example is when Thibault sent a message out to the Seawall team early one morning celebrating our heros, Enrique, and his family. This story also demonstrates what happens when a company has prioritized relationships over transactions and has taken time to care for the people in every facet of the company. Employees invest back into the company that invests in them.

> I got in this morning around 5 a.m., and as I was walking up to our R. House from 28th Street, I saw that all of the lights were on. Thinking that we had forgotten to turn the lights off last night, I continued walking up to the building. As I got closer, I saw Enrique inside, pushing around the fancy Zamboni machine while he cleaned the floor. Instead of going up the stairs to our office, I opened the door to the service corridor that runs behind all the vendors, which was immaculately clean, and walked around to the seating area. Not only was Enrique maneuvering the machine, but

his daughter and son-in-law were busy taking chairs off the tables and setting them back into place. I gave them each a big hug and thanked them for all their help. As I was walking toward the back stairs, I saw Rosa, Enrique's wife, mopping up the bathrooms and stopped to thank her too. They must have gotten there way before 4 a.m. R. House was shining, it was so clean, and it looked as new as it did the first day we opened.

I was so thankful for the behind-the-scenes work that no one ever sees, the work of unsung heroes, that the work the Amaya family does for Seawall every day and, for the behind-the-scenes work that we all do here to keep the company and projects going. I love how flat this organization is and how much we all own the different pieces we work daily.

Deep-rooted appreciation doesn't play by any rules. The field is open, and you can run as far and wide as you like. Go further and higher in your appreciation of others than even you have thought possible. The people who work under our leadership are not here to serve us. It is the other way around—we are here to serve them.

## Deep-Rooted Appreciation through Company Policies

This idea of deep-rooted appreciation can go far beyond words and actions, and indeed, it really must. This style of appreciation can extend even into internal company policies, and in many cases, we adjusted our policies as we learned. It's not simply important; it's imperative that we treat all those working with us as stakeholders in the success of the company, whether they are the cleaning crew or the project managers. As leaders, our job is to ensure that everyone benefits from the perks.

Here's an example of how we overhauled our medical policy years ago to do just that.

Back in 1989, our newly appointed HR director, Kathy Brooks (who previously worked for us in construction administration) brought to my attention that even though we were going for "top-down decency" and a flat company, we were falling short of our own standards in a glaring way within our medical plan.

First, partners in the company got their plan for free, and all of their out-of-pocket costs were reimbursed. Second, let's say it cost $100 total per paycheck to insure one's family; well, that was the price every person paid, whether they were a janitor or a Harvard grad.

Something needed to change. We wanted every person, especially the folks doing the hard and lower-paying work, to be able to insure their families no matter what. If they needed coverage, they should be able to get coverage—great coverage—and it should be affordable. So Kathy put forth a plan, which was fully embraced. Everyone's healthcare cost would be in proportion to their annual salaries. So for coverage, it cost say one percent because one percent of an administrator or maintenance person's salary is not the same as the senior executives. This meant that those who could afford to pay more did and ensured that everyone's healthcare was within their budget.

Surprisingly, the affordable healthcare for employees wasn't just altruistic; it directly helped the company. Our employees were able to come to work daily, knowing that they could take care of their families if and when they were sick. They knew we were integral to this, and that created amazing loyalty and good will. They wanted to work for us, and it was simply more than a job.

Some of those folks maintaining our buildings in Baltimore were the highest tenured employees. Because of their efforts day in and day out, we wanted to take care of them, and as a result, they stayed with us for years. That's what happens when you invest in relationships. That's what happens when you seek ways to bring more decency, dignity, and respect to the people who work with you.

## Inside-Out Leadership in Everyday Life

Deep-rooted appreciation is a trait that must be nurtured to continue to grow and to be fully effective, and that's why it doesn't stop with the workplace. We aren't leaders just some of the time; we are leaders all of the time. We must always be sensitive to the folks hard at work around us, even if they do not work with us. There is never a time when we shouldn't stand up and applaud the unsung heroes.

I remember some time ago when I needed to book a complicated set of flights for my family using frequent flier miles, companion passes, and retail seats. I was exhausted just thinking about the strange web of it all. The Southwest reservationist who helped me was, hands down, off the charts. She took the time to walk me through multiple options before finally implementing the best plan for purchasing. I was so impressed that I noted her name and wrote a letter to the CEO of Southwest praising her. Later, I was thrilled to receive a letter from him in return thanking me and letting me know he had reached out directly to the service representative. I would have loved to have been a fly on the wall when she received acknowledgment from the CEO.

Nurturing appreciation means stopping to acknowledge the folks we see hard at work in public spaces every day, letting them know their work is appreciated and that we see they are doing so much more than just cleaning or bagging groceries. These individuals are making a difference by improving the lives of those around them, and we should let them know. Their smiles are dead giveaways for how much it means to be acknowledged for their daily efforts. Thoughtfulness toward others is a way to honor every human's inherent dignity and worth. A cashier at a grocery store showed me that when she took me totally aback one day with her positive energy.

Her name was Gloria. (I remember because people who work behind registers have name tags for a reason—they are individuals worthy of recognition.) I often find inquiring about the origin of their name to be a great way to initiate conversation and acknowledge the beauty in their personal identity. Anyway, Gloria lifted my tired spirit that evening with her enthusiasm, infectious smile, and inquisitive questions about my day.

I had to thank her. "You've honestly raised my mood and brought a smile to my face!"

"So much to be happy about in this life!" was her reply.

"Glad I could share that with you!"

In what could otherwise be seen as a rote and tedious job, she took ownership of making sure her vibrant attitude passed off to the customers—a gesture I've never since forgotten. Gloria embodied the heart of an inside-out leader.

When relationships are at the center of everything, your impact, and the impact of those working with you will have the greatest payback. If we want to be seen as partners rather than landlords, we must be relationship-driven.

# 5. Inside-Out Company Culture

As you build your team, a major focus must be on developing the strengths of everyone on the team and helping them feel they are contributing equally to the successes of the company.

This idea brings to mind an episode in Malcolm Gladwell's podcast, Revisionist History. In the episode titled "My Little Hundred Million," Gladwell discusses weak links versus strong links. He finds the weak link/strong link connection in sports a good tool for problem-solving in other areas of life, like business or politics, or education. He begins with a book called The Numbers Game, which asks, "What matters more? How good your best player is, or how good your worst player is?"

Basketball is a superstar sport; it's all about how well the best player plays. Whatever you do, don't let the superstar get the ball because if he does—he's going to score. He can take a ball at the backcourt and get it to the front and make a basket all on his own. This is an example of a strong link sport because you can have a player who is only 45% of the best player, and it often doesn't affect the outcome or success of the team. Soccer is the opposite; it's a weak link sport. There are up to eleven players on the soccer field at any given time, and a goal requires a sequence of beautiful plays and passes. Every player is as important as the superstar. You can look at it this way: say your superstar beautifully intercepted a pass and brought the ball back into possession, and then proceeded to start a sequence of eight great passes. Well, if the poorest player gets the ninth pass and botches it—those eight perfect passes mean nothing.

So what does this have to do with an inside-out company culture? I've already expressed the importance of investing in strengths and not weaknesses, which makes it seem like business is probably a strong link connection, and actually, it's not.

Business is best supported when viewed as a weak link connection and that's the basis of the sports analogy. We are only as good as our worst players, which is why it's of the utmost importance to invest in everyone, in every team member.

Like business, an orchestra is a weak link organization. The violin section might be flawless and have some of the most skilled players who can carry the most difficult and intricate melodies, but if the kettle drums can't keep a beat, they're never going to make it to opening night. Making music or exceeding client expectations, an empowered team is behind each. It falls on the shoulders of the conductor to bring teams together in relationship and not competition. It is the leader's responsibility to create an atmosphere of trust and empathy.

The next few sections look at how to transfer inside-out leadership traits and philosophies into a team dynamic. If the leader is faithful to the servant-leader and inside-out ideals, the effect trickles down, and the internal teams operate from those ideals, too, thus creating a truly inside-out company culture.

## Creating an Inside-Out Company Culture

A strong inside-out company culture that is driven by relationships cultivates a spirit of openness and positive energy that support those who execute the important daily functions of the company and help them extend it to everyone they work with. Teams and relationships are synonymous—they drive each other, so when individuals work in teams that value close relationships, they are empowered to rise to their highest potential, and there is more intrinsic motivation to succeed. Individuals in a team get to lean on the collective wisdom of the group which allows them to take their skills to new heights.

## Give Plenty of Rope and Plenty of Grace

An inside-out company culture is one where teams feel the most free and creative in their roles. They feel supported and even expected to speak freely, challenge ideas, provide information, and share their own thoughts and opinions. To really feel that way and do those things, teams need to know that leadership has their back.

Back in my Columbia days, what did it look like to truly have our team members' backs? It took trust, a lot of it, and from right out of the gate. Now, it wasn't a naive trust. We'd already hired people who we believed aligned with the company's vision and who demonstrated a team-centered approach in their work ethic. We were also in close communication with them through one-on-one meetings, so it was an intentional trust.

We believed in giving people plenty of rope.

Does that mean people will make mistakes? Everyone does. As inside-out leaders, we know that mistakes are just learning opportunities, and quite honestly, if those working with us understood the parameters around the financial models for our projects and the kind of numbers we were trying to hit, then they shot for those, and we trusted them not to do anything to ever sink the company. This kind of trust never steered us wrong or put the company under, even when there was a large financial mistake to account for.

I remember when one of our leasing representatives related a story about the time she made her first (and honestly, last) big mistake. She was distraught, felt certain she'd done irreparable harm to the company and worried if her job would be placed on the line. A small miscalculation on her part cost us maybe a dollar more per square foot on a large development. She came to me with her head low, not knowing what to expect. Our Columbia office was still young, and I was getting the hang of this leadership thing, but I knew this woman cared about the company, and I knew it was my job to empower her. So I smiled and asked, "But did you learn anything?" "Oh yes!" she said and went on to describe how she would handle situations like this in the future. I told her, "Perfect. Then you're doing great."

Years later, I would hear a quote from Benjamin Zander, the great New York symphony conductor that captured this attitude perfectly: "When you make a mistake, throw your hands in the air and say, 'How fascinating!'" As I reflect on that situation, that sounds about right.

Our leasing representative left feeling empowered and secure in her job. And I never knew her to miscalculate another project again; she was a terrific asset to our team, and it was right to take the high road that prioritized the relationship over the mistake. More importantly, though, she, and the rest of the team realized on a deeper level that I trusted them to have the smarts to get a job done, and if their judgment was ever in error or they were stuck, they could always come to me for help. It is precisely in moments like these that leaders continue to consciously engineer their purposeful company and reinforce their commitment to relationships.

Another time, I assigned two challenging jobs to Bill Pullin, our team's maintenance person, asking him to put a new roof on a building while the tenant was still inside and to make a parking lot for the tenant. The budget was the same for each project. He brought the two jobs in total about $10,000 over, and the client was so happy with the work and pleased Bill had met the timeframe. When one of the Manekin partners at corporate saw the variance report, they took Bill to task for being over budget. This conversation happened in the hallway, where everyone in the office—including me—could hear it. I didn't waste a moment to intervene. "He's done a great job bringing both of these projects in. There were other significant challenges to meet. Don't just focus on the budget but on a job done well and on time."

Standing up for your team is an important part of leadership's responsibilities; it is our job to protect them and support them and stand on their side. Sometimes we do have to have serious conversations with a team or employee, but we can do it in private to maintain dignity, respect, and the relationship.

Let gentleness lead. If a leader is genial with their teams, their teams will be genial with each other. It's really as simple as that. Just as leaders are always on the lookout for ways to encourage, delight, and inspire their teams, so too must teams always be looking to encourage, delight, and inspire the contractors and vendors they work with as well as their clients and the community at large. They can't do that unless they truly believe that all hands make a difference and that the company stands behind them one hundred percent.

And sometimes having their back is also about helping them clean up their mistakes, no questions asked.

The same maintenance manager was again putting a roof on for a tenant in a very old building. The tenant made and sold high-end men's suits. Our team contracted with a roofing company we'd long trusted, and accidents . . . happen. The roofer made an error in the demo of the roof that wasn't realized until they were pouring hot asphalt into the area. It turned out there were some holes in the metal sheeting that held the roof up. The asphalt oozed right through those holes, into the building, and onto the fancy suits. A significant chunk of merchandise was ruined. The tenant flipped out. He had suits to sell! The roof was a day late! Now this? Instead of waiting for the insurance company to go through all their steps, we wrote the tenant a check right then and there. That's the kind of thing leaders and their teams are willing to do when they truly value the relationship above all else.

Long ago, I read an article in the *Harvard Business Review* that said something to the effect of: if you make a mistake and somehow don't meet your customer's needs, but if you stand up and apologize in a sincere way, and then put some action out in front of you to say, "I am sorry this happened," then you will solidify a much stronger relationship even though you had the conflict. I find this to be true regardless of whether it is a client relationship, an employee relationship, or even a familial relationship—having the humility to stand up, apologize, and take action to right the situation will maintain relationships despite conflicts and is the material of great leadership.

Giving teams and the individuals within them enough rope is about staying connected to them without micromanaging them.

There should be enough slack so that if they get to an edge and fall a couple of hundred feet down, I can still pull them back. The mistake has been made; there might be some damage, but neither the employee nor the company will hit rock bottom. However, if we saw an employee about to trip over a molehill, heck, we let them fall over it and didn't worry about pulling up any slack on the rope. We were comfortable giving those who worked with us a lot of responsibility, even if they were young, even if they were new to this type of work. One young woman, in a role responsible for big decisions and dealing with lots of money in transactions, came to me once with a problem and said, "I'm not quite sure what to do. Do I have to make this decision, or can you?" I looked at her and said, "A bad decision is better than no decision. You make a decision, and then we'll live with the consequences of it."

Of course, I was there to help give her perspective if she wanted and needed it, but it wasn't my job to pull in the rope and make the decision for her. If I did that, I would have taken away her opportunity for growth. We empowered those working with us to learn from their mistakes.

Good leadership is about giving grace for mistakes because mistakes aren't a big deal in the long run. When people do hit the mark, make sure to praise them. Make them feel like they have a hand on the steering wheel—because if we're doing our job right, they do.

## Provide Resources and Opportunities Above and Beyond What Is Expected

Randy Gerwig, owner of Quality Painting, long-time subcontractor of Manekin Corporation, and lifelong friend, shared with me what he does to create a company culture of respect that supports his painters and their ambitions. Back in the mid-'70s, when I first met Randy, his attitude and way of being with his staff inspired me, and I hoped to take a bit of his wisdom and apply it to our company culture. In his own words:

> When I came to Quality Painting, early in December of 1974, I'd left a large company because I was tired of it, and this was a chance to help my dad out. One of the first things I did was put a shuffleboard table and a ping pong table in and fill the soda machine with beer. I wanted our guys to know they were more than painters and that their life was more than painting. I told them, "Look, life is not all about

work, dammit. At the end of the day—if you can—have a beer, play a game of ping pong, hang out together." One day, my dad said, "What are you doing? A pool table and shuffleboard in the shop?"

I said, "We need to do this. I need our guys to stick around."

Randy showed me that creating a company culture that is fun to be a part of, one that celebrates the people working there, is just as important as everything else. And he took it further too; he also recognized the importance of instilling dignity and worth into his employees in other ways.

I also offered health insurance plans to everyone, and the company paid seventy-five percent of the plan. I initiated sick days and holidays. You've got to realize—this was never done in the painting industry. The thinking was, "Yeah, yeah, painters. Hire 'em. Fire 'em. Who gives a shit?" But I disagreed. Other companies might dock a painter's pay if they came in with too much paint on their clothes. "You're supposed to put that on the wall," they'd say. I wanted to change the stigma that painters were a dime a dozen.

I told our guys, "Be proud of what you do. Put on clean clothes; go into McDonald's with clean clothes—not covered in paint. Hold your head high. Present yourself with dignity."

And we paid our guys above industry standards. My dad always said, "If you're not paying someone what they're worth, in two weeks, you will be." They will slow down to that pace. I wanted it to be different. I didn't care what other companies were doing. That didn't matter to me. I wanted this one to be different. We weren't the cheapest contractors, but there are people who pay for top-notch folks, and that's what we had. That's because we didn't treat them as laborers but as painters—professional painters. When you do that, the cream rises to the top.

Randy was always looking for opportunities to invest in those working with him and to provide opportunities and resources that would support them to excel in both their personal and professional lives.

I remember one time Ricky came to me because we'd just hired a Latino guy (who is still with us to this day).

"Hey Randy," he said, "this guy is aces. He can speak English, French, and Spanish. And he's a natural! He paints really good. What do you want to do?"

I said, "Buy him a truck."

Ricky said, "We can't afford that!"

And I said, "We can't afford not to."

We made our shop and its tools and resources available to our guys. That might sound crazy because people don't usually encourage side work from their painters, but I did. I said, "If you want to make extra money on the side, I will let you borrow ladders, trucks, and you can buy your paint on our account to save some pennies. If that is what it takes to do better, I want everyone here to do better. I don't want to come in here and see someone downtrodden because this is what we do for a living." Consequently, one of the guys took advantage of the resources and saved up to buy a house in the country, and now he races race horses! It can be done!

And, of course, Randy knew more about celebrating the unsung hero than almost anyone else I knew. He taught me that good leaders never forget the importance of taking even the smallest and sincerest of actions to show appreciation for their teams.

> One day, it was 120 degrees, and I walked onto a job site and saw my crew spraying steel.
>
> "Holy mackerel," I thought, "how are they doing it?"
>
> But they were doing it. They were doing so good, and I didn't know how I could thank them enough. At break time, I went down to the bank and got ten one-hundred-dollar bills and then went around stuffing the bills in their pockets. They never forgot that. Ever. Did it help get the job done? Of course, but they were doing an amazing job anyway. I just wanted to recognize them for it

Randy created an inside-out company culture through and through. He did everything within his power as a leader to make sure that his crew not only had the resources to satisfy the company's goals but also to satisfy their own. It just goes to show that the two are not mutually exclusive. Sometimes, to do this, we must call upon the intuitive nature of leadership.

Good leaders seek to understand the individual person beyond black and white.

You can see how this might be done in this example from Kathy, who moved from working in administration to HR. After working with Kathy for many years, I knew instinctively that she had what it would take to assume an HR role in the company. Although her degree wasn't in HR, she was a people person first and foremost. Learning the technical skill sets of HR would be easy for her. Most importantly, I knew she would be responsive on a human level with those in the company. However, this wasn't a career path she had ever considered for herself. She didn't know what it entailed. The following is Kathy's account of her experience of the dinner we had when I offered her the change in careers:

Today, I still work for Manekin but in a totally different role.

Somewhere in 1990, the real estate market took a turn, and I moved from construction administration to a sales position, but I wasn't as happy there. Donald said, "Can I take you out to dinner?" I said, sure. I had a couple of bourbon and Cokes and was feeling relaxed, and he says, "Listen, we don't have the means to keep this sales position anymore or keep providing the training you need for it. However, I would like to transition you into a human resources position. I think you'd be fantastic at that." I was like, what do human resources even do? But I jumped right on it, knowing the company would support me, and I loved working here. I have been in HR ever since. It's a perfect fit. I went to college to be a nurse because I wanted to nurture people but came out with an analytical degree in stats. So you see, HR is the perfect blend of both analytical and nurturing. I had no idea it was even a job choice or that I would like it, but Donald was able to figure out that this was where I should go. He knew my strengths, and he was invested in me. I never would have gotten there without him. It was a home run for me, and I hope a good decision for the company. Having been here this long, I've done it well.

While helping every individual satisfy their personal goals often means your company benefits from less turnover and a more fulfilling company culture, the following story shows that taking care of people sometimes means they end up finding greater success for themselves outside of the company. And that's good too. That fits under the banner of inside-out leadership.

Bill Pullin worked in the Columbia office and was the team member responsible for maintenance. He was sharp at seeing beyond problems to find solutions. It seemed like he could respond and fix tenant requests before they'd even hung up the phone. He was an incredible asset to our team. Below, Bill shares his experience at Manekin Corporation:

> Ray Blank was a company consultant, a sharp businessperson, and one intimidating guy. But Donald set up for me to spend time with him once or twice a week for a couple of years, and those meetings went far to empower me in my role with the company and in the decades after when I ran my own business. I remember the first time I met Ray. He and Donald had a conversation about helping me finish my degree if I wanted to. See, I'd left college after two and a half years to support my family. We brainstormed together, and based on my interests, passion, and talents, we collectively decided that school actually wouldn't support me as well as to keep doing what I was doing and to get more on-site training. I worked hard for them for six and a half years before I became interested in starting my own company. Now, I had come from nothing, no money, no assets, nothing. But Manekin empowered me to take the reins of my personal goals and start pulling them. It took a couple of years, but I put it all together. I brought in a finance guy. I got the company off the ground, started making money, and then brought a partner on, and have been doing that ever since. I credit Donald and Ray for encouraging me to do that even though it wasn't in the company's best interest. From my time at the company, I learned how to be a leader and how I wanted to operate in my own business. Those things—trusting my teams, treating them well, empowering them are the hallmark of my business now too.

Inside-out leadership is a way of being that creates great success for one's business, but it's not exclusively about personal business success at all. It's one hundred percent always about helping others succeed no matter what. Providing Bill these opportunities to see his future personified that it's 100% about helping people succeed.

## Strike a Balance and Throw Out the Rule Book

Those in leadership roles have always been adamant about supporting those working with us to strike a home-work-life balance, and it's up to leadership to practice what we preach for others to trust that they really can put their home life first when they need to. As leaders we need to see and appreciate the whole person and their needs beyond just what might be in the company manual. When our daughter or son was in a school play, I left early to see them perform, and I encouraged those working with us to do the same with their own families. They didn't need to ask permission—they could just go. People should feel that if they need to take a sick day or need a day to take care of their sick child or sick parent, they are free and fully supported to just do it. If they are sick or need to tend to someone—let them call in. It doesn't matter if they have used up all their sick days in the company policy. If they need more, they can have it. Trust them not to abuse that freedom, and they won't. They will take the time they need, not more, and everything will flow efficiently and harmoniously. Our company took an even bigger leap of faith and didn't even have a sick leave policy. If you were sick, you called in sick. Simple as that.

Our role as leaders is to get the best of those working with us and inspire them to take on more. Recognizing that life happens and that it doesn't always happen in neat and tidy boxes means being flexible with our policies, rules, and expectations. It is of the utmost importance that the atmosphere in the company should allow for exceptions.

In fact, I'm all about getting rid of rule books altogether.

We didn't have a rule book. We firmly believed in treating people how we, ourselves, wished to be treated. We imagined the kind of work atmosphere we'd like to be in and where we would thrive. And so, that's why we didn't write one. What we've learned is that if we simply treat those working with us as the capable, intelligent, goodwill people we believed them to be, then they rise to the occasion and err on the side of what's right. People blossom when they are trusted to do what's right. In business, there are certainly important regulations and procedures that must be followed. Say for example, specific forms for healthcare must be filled out and filed. OK, follow the procedure so claims can be processed expeditiously and with the right information. For the policies and procedures that deal with personal happiness and what is happening in one's family—then there are exceptions to every rule depending on the circumstance.

Take dress code, for example. We didn't need to create rules or policies telling people what to wear coming into work. Everyone came in looking professional. It never even crossed my mind that something could be written down stating the appropriate way to dress for our company. It never occurred to me that the people we brought on board wouldn't dress professionally for the work they were doing. It was our trust in them and our lack of rules that created a safe and nurturing space for people.

Even when things went south with certain employees, we treated them with dignity and respect. If we needed to let someone go, we'd say: "You're obviously not happy, and it's not working for either of us, and we want you to be happy. So here is severance, and if you believe it would be helpful, we are offering you a career transitioning specialist so you can understand yourself better and what kind of work fits you. We want you to be able to find the right position in the right company. Go find a job where you feel you're a great fit." This isn't hard to do, and it doesn't take much money to do either. Relationships, even the ones that are ending, are more valuable than the money.

And an inside-out leader invests in people unconditionally.

## Strategies for Bringing Teams Together in Relationship

In the 1980s, a strategy called Management by Walking Around, or MBWA, was popularized by Tom Peters and Robert H. Watermen in their book, *In Search of Excellence: Lessons from America's Best-Run Companies*. The term is still widely used today. What the two men found was that companies in which the CEOs and managers spent more time in the field than behind a desk were the most successful because they were the most aware of what was happening in their company and better able to problem solve with their teams. Their idea supports my own personal belief, learned in the classroom, that we can be of most value when we're in the thick of things. A good use of time is to be present, available, and visible—in other words, take intentional but impromptu walks around. This will give you both a bird's eye view—a view of the trees in the forest—and allow you to listen and observe more intentionally. Management by walking around is a deliberate and genuine strategy for staying abreast of people's work, interests, and ideas, and it requires that leaders possess a range of skills including active listening, observation, recognition, and appraisal. It brings participation, spontaneity, and informality to the idea of open-door management.

For me, getting out there and being with people, listening and observing, engaging on their level, was my singular purpose. I wanted to be with my team, with Bill in the truck witnessing and listening to the maintenance issues he was working on, with David, Lewis, and Ellen in their leasing efforts, David or Paul walking the construction jobs, and Karen, Kathy, Leslie, and Ginger in administration and accounting. These were the people putting forth the vision of the company. I didn't want to be removed from that. I wanted to be with them, rubbing elbows on a daily basis. I was most often an observer, taking in all that was being accomplished. In doing so, I could better offer my thoughts and help them determine which direction they wanted to go.

And again, by getting out there myself, I was setting an example for the other team leaders to do the same. A little thing I often tried to do before the workday got going was to show up around 6 a.m. in front of our rental properties and help the ground crews pick up trash. If you're managing by walking around, I don't think it's enough to just stand around and watch people. It's important to be a part of the action, to show solidarity and that we're all in this together.

Members of the team, on their own initiative, started getting together early on snow days to help the maintenance team shovel tenant sidewalks. Now, shoveling sidewalks was not in their job description. There was no expectation to do such a thing, but they loved the company, and they loved coming together and helping each other out whenever they could. We all were in the same boat rowing together. There was no such wording as "It's not my job."

When those working with you see you rowing too, it brings out the best in them.

## Support Teams with Trainings and Consultants

The company also spent a lot of time and resources training people, and we didn't only train for the nuts and bolts of the job, the black and white of "here's what you need to do today or tomorrow." We trained our teams how to think and how to *feel*. And this wasn't accomplished by lectures but through daily actions. For new folks coming on board with Manekin in its commercial developments in Columbia, they would ride shotgun. Together we'd go see the buildings—understanding each building and what it offered. We'd meet existing tenants and with brokers to hear their perspectives. Our new hires would observe how we moved companies from suspect to prospect to tenant. One time, we had two new employees go to several residential developments in Baltimore and pretended to be potential residents. This on-site experience gave them real insight into how it feels to interact with leasing agents. In many cases, they felt they were treated more like a transaction than as a relationship. They would take copious notes after each visit to remember what they observed and learned. These visits gave them the platform to develop their own relationship-based interactions with those residents who came to Seawall's developments. Teaching the rote skills of real estate, like how to prepare a letter of intent, do a credit check, or draw up a lease, is easy. But the ability to make a tenant feel welcomed, the wherewithal to remember a client's birthday and send a card, the ability to get someone over to your opinion without being offensive—these require a different sort of skillset and training that's best learned in the moment and often through leaders walking around and cultivating a culture of relationship.

One of the best places to train people how to feel and how to build relationships was also in team meetings.

The purpose of the weekly meeting was to bring everyone together for an hour or so with no predetermined agenda. Everyone came in and created the agenda as to what they wanted to talk about. In reality, not everyone was on the same page. Ray Blank taught me that what we needed was to reach decisions through consensus. So, we stayed until everyone agreed to what we were going to do and how we were going to do it. With everyone sharing ideas, it sometimes took a bit of time to reach a unanimous decision that let us move forward. And coming together in consensus was critical. Simply taking a vote, without having engaged in the conflict of ideas and conversation, wouldn't have bred camaraderie or the best ideas.

The best ideas and the best answers are always found by team efforts. This reality is described in NASA's "Survive on the Moon" exercise, which asks individuals to rank fifteen objects for moon survival. When I used this exercise with the MBA students I led at Johns Hopkins University, they ranked just 60% correctly, according to NASA's criteria, when working as individuals. But when I had them work in teams of three to four, they were able to correctly rank 90%. The team collaboration meant there was a conflict of ideas, and those ideas got to be expressed, aired, debated, and in the end—they came up with the most complete and correct answers.

Teams working together are more effective at getting proper answers through consensus than just taking a vote and saying, well, it's five to four, so we are going to make this decision. You will always have four unhappy people in that scenario-four people who just have to go along with it and do it. In our team meetings, we had to do what was in the best interest of the group and not what was in the best interest of just four or five people. The beauty of the team meetings was to provide opportunity for healthy discussions and a full airing of ideas. At the end of every meeting, we went around, and each person got to share if the meeting met their expectation and if it was worth their effort. We didn't dismiss the meeting after coming to a consensus; we continued to listen to people critique the meeting.

We also invested in an on-site time management consultant named Michael Bryant, who people liked to call a corporate psychiatrist. He was available to our teams and met with each person one-on-one, once a week, then once every other week, and then once a month, helping them prioritize and be the best they could be—more effective, efficient, and therefore even more enthusiastic about the work they were doing. By making plenty of resources available to teams, they will be continually supported to be the best that they can be and to turn around and give their best back to achieving the company's goals, which in our case has always been about maintaining the kind of relationships that exceed all expectations.

For example, Kathy Brooks shared how she was more than just an employee waiting for direction. If she had an idea, leadership was there to empower and support her.

"The company atmosphere made my job in HR so fun and rewarding. In my role, employees confided in me and let me know what was going on with them on a personal level and came to me when they needed support. That happened because I was an extension of this wonderful company, which then allowed me to be a "Fairy Godmother." I could simply ask Donald, or any partner, for whatever an employee needed help with. There was never a time that I was told "no." It certainly wasn't a case of any employee's whim or fancy being met; I was able to ferret those out and minimize expectations there. It was about the real stuff, the important stuff, that I was truly able to be in it with them on behalf of the company. We didn't make a big deal or embarrass them, but we'd help them any way we could, whether it was a small financial loan or making the call to a facility because they needed some rehab, or their wife did, or they had an anorexic child. Then we could say, I know a program let us help you. Those moments and that support is imprinted on employees and is not forgotten. HR is often seen as a function to reprimand, punish, and recite rules. Our HR function was not feared and was immensely trusted to help when necessary. The "client" for me was our employees, and as with all our clients our goal was to exceed their expectations as well."

# 6. Vendors and Contractors: The External Team

Vendors and contractors are as much a part of the company's team as those who work "in-house," and they also need to feel their importance and connection to the higher purpose. It is only because of them and their efforts that a project will be able to exceed the expectations of those you serve.

The next story—and the others in this chapter—all come from Randy Gerwig, who I introduced earlier, and who started subcontracting with Manekin Corporation in the very beginning of our Columbia office days. The value of his stories is in how you can truly see how crucial trust and respect and deep-rooted appreciation are to vendors and contractors and why we must extend the company culture to include them as well.

> "One time, I walked on a job where two guys got in a fight over a girl, and one guy threw the other completely through a wall. I'm walking the job with Donald and he sees the collapsed wall, but he doesn't say a word, not one word. He knew I'd take care of it. The next day, it was fixed. We had a mutual trust. We knew we had each other's backs. Walking another job one day, he looked around and said, 'You're not doing so well on this job, are ya?' And I just said, "Yeah." Donald said, 'I'll put some extra money in for you.' Who the hell does that? Contractors don't do that. But Donald did."

Inside-out leadership depends upon everyone—especially subcontractors—feeling like stakeholders in the company and in the project.

Relationships drive purposeful companies, and a company's reach extends far beyond its own office doors, which means so must its commitment to relationships. Second to my father, no one has taught me more about celebrating those behind the scenes and prioritizing relationships over transactions than Randy. His stories will come into play many times in this chapter as I call on his insights to help describe how to invest in your external teams and why it is so worth it.

First, we're going to go further back to a real-world classroom experience I had right after I joined my family's development business. This meeting shaped how we would carry out the construction portion at Manekin in all of the Columbia developments. Jack Dreisch, a principal in the construction company, Northern Chesapeake Builders, had called a round table of subcontractors to meet with our lead architect and seasoned associates from Manekin Corporation (I was the new kid on the block that day). We were discussing how we'd just finalized a long-term lease with The Columbia Medical Plan for their entire 30,000-square-foot office building and how they had a short window to have the work finished. The subcontractors at the table would be charged with its actual construction. With my naive understanding, I thought they were there to discuss the bidding. I was expecting something serious and assumed the contractors would be reserved and do whatever they were told. But that wasn't what happened. Jack was a powerful presence, and not in a forceful way; he had strength and conviction, and he led that round table like the grand patriarch of a congenial family. He even sat in the middle of the table, a leader surrounded and engaged with his team.

The collaboration and energy were palpable. Everyone contributed their perspective and described how their work would evolve and relate to Jack's overall objectives. It was the most absorbing business meeting I could have imagined. I learned those subcontractors had been with Jack for years and had been rewarded year after year with more work-and not because they were the lucky ones with the lowest bid! It was because they delivered time after time. When everything was hashed out at the end, the deals were completed with a handshake—not paperwork. I craved that same team spirit and camaraderie in our company—I wanted our subcontractors to come together around one table and know they were all in one boat rowing together with us.

Not only did that kind of relationship seem inviting and rewarding and make for long-lasting partnerships, but I learned soon after that, it also makes for better communication and deliverables. And that was crucial because the vendor's responsiveness to clients is critical.

David Kinne, who led our construction efforts, remembered the following story where the strength of our partnerships was truly seen and felt, and vendor responsiveness proved unparalleled.

> We were two weeks away from turning over the keys of a new building to a software defense company. Everything was ready; even the carpet was down. All that was left was to open the seemingly endless miles of landscape furniture and install it over a 55,000-square-foot cubicle office space. Simple. But then a sprinkler joint in a ceiling line blew around 1 a.m. Luckily, a couple of painters were on site doing touch-ups and they called the superintendent for the job, who called up the team's maintenance coordinator, Bill. When Bill and his team got there, water was pouring off the loading dock in the rear and even out the front doors. They made some calls. A dozen people from two different subcontracting teams just showed up—in the middle of the night. They got the water shut off and spent until dawn pulling up the carpet and getting it out of the way. Drywall was damaged four feet up the walls; it all had to be cut off and replaced. Everything had to be repainted. We needed new carpet. And we needed it all in two weeks. But the furniture was undamaged. What happened next was extraordinary. Everyone pitched in to get things back on track: subcontractors, bosses, field people, office people, everyone! No one stood around giving orders; everyone just helped. They didn't have to, but they did. It was a tremendous effort only made possible by people coming together for a higher purpose as one unified team.

Life happens, and projects do not always go according to plan and that's OK. They don't have to because you will be surrounded by the people you built strong relationships with who are willing to go above and beyond for you just like you've always gone above and beyond for them. This symbiotic relationship has extraordinary potential for exceeding the expectations of those you serve and making a lasting impact on your community.

## Building the External Team

The existing system, back then, for constructing spaces at Manekin was functional at best. We would gather our prospect's space requirements and send those to an architect. The architect would prepare drawings. Then we would send the drawings to a general contractor, who would then send the drawings to subcontractors. Many days later, we would receive a pricing bid from each of the subcontractors. After Jack's meeting, I realized that our system was causing us to lose valuable time and didn't offer any opportunity to build intimacy and work hand in hand with our prospects and contractors. Jack inspired me to rethink the process.

The change unfolded by first identifying and personalizing our relationships with individual contractors: the plumbers, mechanical engineers, drywall installers, painters, electricians, etc. I met with them individually and shared our higher purpose. Manekin wanted to be seen as fully responsive neighbors in Howard County, visible partners in the success of those we developed for and in the county, both in terms of economic development and quality of life. Because of that, I communicated with the contractors that our higher purpose meant always going above and beyond and exceeding the expectations of our clients. I told the contractors that as we grew and formed partnerships, we hoped they would want to share this vision for the combined success for the companies we served and for their own company. In essence, I invited them to be stakeholders in the vision and key players on our team.

Then it was time to meet collectively and switch roles—I was a student; they were teachers. What ideas did they have to make this new kind of collaboration a success? As I had hoped, ideas flew. One of the most valuable and long-lasting ideas was how they each came up with pricing scenarios, allowing our office to estimate costs of work quickly, saving us valuable time and allowing us to be more responsive to the clients we were courting. Being responsive to the client, they said, had as great of a value for their own companies as it did for us. The contractors said they'd work collectively to get work done and without using change orders—unless the scope changed—and that they would do whatever they needed to do to guarantee we always met completion dates. All they asked of us was to prepare the schedule of work, deliver the drawings and anticipated occupancy date, and then—stand back.

We decided that once work commenced, we'd all meet weekly to review the schedule and work through any issues that arose in the field. Yet because of these heightened relationships and team integration, the amazing workers, the unsung heroes within these contracting teams ended up resolving most day-to-day issues without ever needing to bring it to the weekly meeting for intervention.

As Randy Gerwig related, "Donald brought everyone around a table each Tuesday, and you looked at each other. Many times, I didn't know who the plumber was, but on Tuesday, I did! Every trade sat at that table. When Donald ran a meeting, and we got to know each other, that visibility led to accountability. At the table, you can't hide, and you learn to respect each other. We never put our paint supplies on the carpets after that, and the plumbers never put their tools against a wet wall. If a plumber put a hole in the wall that I had to fix, he wasn't hiding; he was right across the table. When it started clicking that we were a team, what was cool was everyone's productivity level started going up! Respect came from those relationships. Some of the friendships I made around that table have lasted these forty years."

Things were all sounding very good to us, and I insisted it had to be a two-way relationship. It was critical to provide these companies with something in return for their Herculean efforts, and the biggest reward Manekin could offer was ongoing work—and we weren't interested in the lowest price, only in exceeding the expectations of our clients, and pay almost before their invoices hit our desks. And by utilizing the same team of subcontractors, we saved a lot of time, not needing to send a project out to bid every time. We all got more work and faster.

This new system was transformational. Suddenly, there wasn't an occupancy date or scope of work we couldn't meet for the tenants we were building for. We were working toward the same prize. Randy Gerwig once said, "Whether we truly were a part of the Manekin team or not, eh, it didn't matter because Donald made us feel like we were. It lived in all of us, every trade, plumbers, electricians, painters, all. He was accessible. He never walked by anyone without introducing himself and saying hi. That was a big, big deal to us because we were used to the big wheels coming on to job sites and just going right by us. Some think the word subcontractor is exactly who we were—sub or beneath. But Donald was different. He treated us different."

## Rallying Against the Odds

Gary Glissan, Vice President and Executive Director for Man-Tech, a national company that provides innovative solutions in cybersecurity and data analysis for the US government, shared that, right from the start, he had a gut feeling about our company. The initial contact he had with everyone in the organization made him feel that we, collectively, really cared about Man-Tech being in our development. Still, it was with some trepidation that he signed—he knew we'd have our work cut out for us. We were constructing Man-Tech's 34,000-square-foot building with just the exterior walls in place and had to have it ready for occupancy in just two months' time. Gary knew that on the sidelines was the leading competitor for the job—one of the best-known developers in the area—and they had already tried to pitch an existing building that only needed customizing and finishing. As Gary shared, "the pressure became severe when one of the principals in the competing development company called my board chairman to say that what Manekin was promising couldn't be done." Nevertheless, Gary dug in his heels, stuck by his choice, and prayed it was the right one.

Meanwhile, our internal and external teams got wind of the heightened stakes, how the other developer said it couldn't be done, and you've never seen people get into gear so fast. We never, for one moment, thought this couldn't be done. Implementing Jack Dreisch's strategy of using the same team of subcontractors, we saved valuable time by eliminating the need to send the job out to bid. The standard interior work crew of up to fifteen people more than tripled, and crews worked ten-hour days, six days per week.

Gary's impression of us and gut instincts held true. What we did for him wasn't anything extra or special. As David Kinne, who led our construction team, once said, "Some people thought we must have been 'up to something,' but what we were up to was simply doing what we said we'd do!"

On the day of the ribbon-cutting ceremony, Gary stood before the gathered guests and said, "It's been the kind of love affair you want to have with your landlord because it makes life easier. It's almost too good to be true. It's an amazing operation. They run their real estate development business the way I'd like to think I run ours."

Our external team rallied against the odds, and you can bet, at the completion of this project, we threw them a big celebration to recognize their incredible work and commitment to the higher purpose.

## Beyond Transactions

As inside-out leaders, we also have the ability to create lasting relationships by eliminating the transactional approach. Just like it takes trusting your internal team to know their roles and do their job, it also takes trusting your contractors to do the same. We subcontracted with some of the same companies for twenty-five years or more. We trusted them because we knew we were aligned together with our purpose. We counted on everyone around the table to do their job, and we never told them what their job was. We were all inextricably tied together in our mutual successes.

Although we were conscious of making sure we were on budget, it was never about the money with the contractors. The role of the leader, like the orchestra conductor, is to know clearly what the music should sound like and to empower the musicians to take responsibility to make sure the music receives a standing ovation at the end. Our contractors played their roles fantastically and we applauded all their efforts.

I went so far as to remove conversations about money from our weekly progress meetings too. The subcontractors didn't need to know about the deals being written or whether the jobs were on budget; we just needed to talk straight about the progress of the job. At meetings like these, it was always about hearing about the progress, working through particular issues, and talking about work coming up. We never said, "Pick up the pace!" or "Do this; do that!" It was always about remembering to do the little things that nurture a solid relationship and make those working with you feel like what they do really matters. For instance, on the agenda sheet that we passed around, we were sure to include everyone's name, and as a first order of business at the meeting, we always introduced everyone to each other if there were new people.

Show deep-rooted appreciation as you lead meetings with your contractors and vendors and watch the ripple effect.

I remember Randy Gerwig sharing with me "that without these troops, we aren't going anywhere." That's why it's of the utmost importance that, as leaders, we go above and beyond to recognize and give credit to our teams. If we don't do it, who will? How else will they ever know that they are a valuable and integral part of the team, that they make a difference, and are critical to the project's success? It was Randy who initiated the first of what would become our yearly holiday contractor party. He brought a grill down to where three or four subcontractors were finishing a project and started grilling hot dogs and hamburgers. Then, David Kinne, who led our construction efforts, brought down a bunch of oysters and proceeded to shuck them. Someone else brought beer.

It was informal, and it stuck. We got to the point where we were sending out 400-500 invitations every year, and the guest list's most important invitees were the workers. We strung lights in warehouse spaces we had developed, set up a Spot-a-Pot, and served oysters, shrimp, and beer. We partied until the kegs ran dry and not a single shellfish was left. I, along with other members of the Columbia team, would move through the guests and thank each person individually. As time went on, we worked with our contractors, and collectively, we anted up the party to not only celebrate our collective success but the communities where we developed. This was a turning point. It was the ripple of our initial efforts years earlier to bring our external team into relationship with us, to row in the same direction toward a higher purpose. The contractors we worked with decided to demonstrate how they had internalized that purpose and made it their own. Together with the contractors, we were connecting their individual efforts to something far greater. A fund was set up in the memory of our dear Karen Dean, who redefined the concept of exceeding expectations and who was dearly loved by all who knew her. Along with every contractor, we contributed to the fund, and from the collections, we made grants to nonprofits in the jurisdictions where we had developments. The grant recipients came forward at the holiday party to accept their grant and share their work with the audience. Together, we were making our communities a better place to live and work. Collectively we believed, isn't this how business should always be?

# Section Three

*Awakening Possibilities*

# 7. It's All About What's Possible

Benjamin Zander, the orchestra director, says that "our job as leaders is to awaken possibility in others." When people awaken to possibility, it is obvious and easy for us to witness it happening in them. But if we aren't seeing it, then we need to ask ourselves, why not?

Throughout the previous chapters, the underlying themes have been about vision, and about having a higher purpose, and empowering others; and that all for the sake of nurturing relationships is the surest foundation for exceeding expectations. When every action a leader takes is in alignment with these aspirations, then their vision becomes contagious. When those around us catch on to the importance of a higher purpose, they immediately see their thought process and actions as part of something bigger than themselves. Gandhi said, "Happiness is when what you think, what you say, and what you do are in harmony." As leaders, we should always be questioning if what we think, say, and do are in harmony because this is the best way to live a sincere life with the greatest power to affect positive change. This is the moment when we can witness and help draw forth the extraordinary potential inherent in each other—in every proposal, in every project, and in every outcome. And it's a great way to spread more joy to the workplace, which also happens to be one of the best motivators for high performance and optimum productivity.

When I talk about seeing beyond in order to see what is possible, what I am really talking about is, of course, using the imagination. The imagination is strengthened only by positive use and should never be left to lie dormant. A strong imagination is key to business success when it comes to exceeding client expectations. The thing is, one must begin by thinking *positively* about the possibilities for a project in order to set a course toward a natural process of success. In thinking and acting with positive intention, we as leaders always take the high road and choose to nurture positivity within ourselves and those around us. If we do, then it follows that all of our words and actions will be in alignment, and we will be able to create an empowering and positive ambiance within our company culture as well-the kind of ambiance that supports the extraordinary potential of the people served and the projects undertaken.

I have had the unique privileges of sitting on the Teach for America advisory board in Baltimore, founding the Foundation for Rural Education in Maryland, and serving as the interim chief operating officer for the Baltimore City Public Schools. In these roles, I have learned that school systems can be, very often and unfortunately, embedded in bureaucracy. As a leader in the education sector, I hoped to awaken those I worked with to new possibilities, new ways of thinking, being, and acting. I took the opportunity to spread what's possible.

I believe most people set out in life to be positive. Many people have told me they wish to create meaning and opportunity for others, and they have learned that to do so that they need their thoughts—their conscious belief systems—to be in line with that thinking too. This allows them to take the necessary actions to exceed the expectations of those around them. Their life, then, is in harmony.

As leaders, if we live our lives in harmony, then we can create harmony around us. And to do so, we must always be stepping back and looking at ourselves objectively and asking—what are my unconscious belief systems, and do they serve the company's higher purpose? You can identify the power of these belief systems simply by witnessing how your body reacts to positive thoughts and actions. A mind anchored in positivity creates a different swell of blood in the body, a surge of vitality for the work to be done. When we imagine possibilities, the effect is physical—there is energy and excitement in the body, both of which go a long way in creating heartfelt projects that exceed expectations. And exceeding the expectations of those we serve is, of course, the ultimate end goal of a purposeful company.

For myself, I have come to appreciate that I alone cannot always figure out the answers to problems that arise (many are issues that I could never possibly know because they are not in my field of expertise), but I can consider the possibility that there are others who could step in to help and lead, those who might have the answers to what our company is planning. One positive belief system I carry that helps me imagine solutions for difficult situations is this: there are always stakeholders that want to be of value to you and assist you in your actions and proposed outcomes.

## Neither Rain nor Snow

If we want to go somewhere, we must create (or imagine) products and services for the potential they could have. As you'll see in the following story from my time serving within the school system, the potential to create an extraordinarily efficient and sustainable mail delivery system was there all along. It took reaching outside ourselves and asking others for help to unlock it.

Within any school system, it falls on some person and team to take responsibility for mail delivery. For Karen, who ran logistics in the Baltimore Public School System, the responsibility was hers, and she found the task of managing a fleet of trucks needing to deliver daily mail to 186 buildings completely overwhelming. I imagine she wasn't alone in that feeling. As a leader, what could I do to help Karen? From the inside-out approach we've been discussing, I helped align her to a higher purpose, made her feel like I was part of the team, and empowered her in her role, but still, none of these things solved the problem of what to do with all that mail! As a leader, I still had a duty to make sure I was giving her all the resources she needed to be successful in her role, and that required taking a step back to ask, "What's possible? Do I know anything about mail delivery? Sure don't." But it just so happened I sat on the United Way board, and one of the other board members was the district manager for UPS.

After one of the board meetings, I started my conversation with him, saying, "All you do every day is get parcels shipped from point A to point B and even perhaps returned as expeditiously as possible. The school system presently has neither an efficient strategy for doing so nor the knowledge of what's required to develop one. Do you think UPS could bring their expertise to bear and come and help us out?"

Without hesitation, he said for sure. He called up the California office, and UPS was thrilled to send a team out who then spent weeks one-on-one with Karen and her team developing a plan and a routing system that worked. She shared with me that she thought she'd died and gone to heaven. All of a sudden, she had a system in place that was off the charts and miles beyond anything she could have envisioned on her own. The time was generously and graciously offered by UPS for free; they never asked for a dime in consulting fees. UPS offered to help because they thought it was the right thing to do for the school system. They care about making a difference in public education, so they did not hesitate to take this opportunity to have a direct impact.

As a leader, you don't need to have all the answers, though you do need to be humble enough to recognize that you don't have all the answers. Be willing to look outside of yourself and call on the help of those around you who would like nothing else than to be a stakeholder in your success, and in this case, the success of a larger community.

## Augmented or Potential Products and Services

Let's take a look at three ways to view business products or services and their potential for exceeding expectations. This will give us both the groundwork and a vocabulary for discussing concepts and philosophies in the rest of the chapter, namely, awakening possibility in our clients and unlocking extraordinary potential in everyone and everything—just like Karen and the mail.

Ted Levitt, the former editor of the *Harvard Business Review* and author of bestselling book *The Marketing Imagination*, among many others, has had a profound effect on my approach to business. In an article titled,

"Marketing Success through Differentiation-of Anything," he offers the most inspiring idea—that potential products or services should only be limited by the imagination and the budget.

Let's take a step back for just a moment to define what Levitt means by "augmented and potential products and services." You are probably familiar with at least the first two types of products/services listed below, but it is in the third and fourth where the true magic lies.

> **Generic:** A generic product is the fundamental or the rudimentary thing needed to set the stakes for a business endeavor. In real estate, the generic products would be the buildings developed.

To move beyond a generic product, a vision is needed. Columbia and Seawall's vision was to be neighbors and stakeholders in the success of those we built for and the communities where we developed. This moves us to the expected.

> **Expected:** The expected product or service is the minimum of what the client expects, that which is absolutely necessary for our product to be viewed as complete in the eyes of end users and the communities we serve.

The minimum expectations to rent an apartment would be: do the heating and A/C provide adequate comfort? Do the dishwasher and laundry machines work? For an office space, minimal requirements include: is it easy for employees and visitors to find parking? Can I occupy the space beyond the 9–5 workday? Is the building secure?

These are all reasonable expectations, and as leaders, as stakeholders in the success and happiness of those we serve—we can do better than just what is expected. Ted Levitt makes the point that "differentiation is not limited to giving the customer just what they expect. What they expect may be augmented by things they never thought about."

**Augmented:** Simply put, augmented services require thinking "outside the box," offering something greater than what the customer ever expected. This might be a surprise "extra" or simply an above-and-beyond energy and mentality.

**Potential:** These are the products and services that should get all of us out of bed in the morning. As described by Levitt, the potential product or service should be anything that first attracts and, most importantly, retains and grows the customer base. It should only be limited by the imagination and the budget.

Potential services live in the world of possibility. Here is where we have the opportunity to create a truly extraordinary experience for the customer because the only real limits are in the mind of the provider. "Things they never thought about," in Levitt's words, equals awakening possibility. Inside-out leaders can and must always be asking, "What if?" and "What's possible?" from ourselves, those working with us, and others. It is only when we look beyond what is expected of our services that we can build the kind of meaningful relationships, which are at the heart of our purposeful company.

Do you remember the story in the introduction about Patch Adams and the patient in the psychiatric hospital? How many fingers do you see? Look beyond what's right in front of you (the expected) and imagine a whole new world of possibilities (the potential). Choose to dwell in a world of possibility, a place of positivity and hope, and you'll find an endless reservoir of energy to draw from that will nourish every encounter, action, and step you take as a leader. I like to view the augmented and potential as a playground of sorts. On this playground, we have opportunities to consistently surprise and delight those we serve.

One of my favorite examples comes from a time during my Manekin Corporation years when we successfully converted a prospect into a client through a rather unconventional approach.

## Taking Possibilities to New Heights, Literally

I have learned that when people have autonomy in their work, they come in extraordinarily happy because they know they have the capability and approval to get out there and really make things happen. And like we discussed above, happiness breeds energy that can be harnessed to awaken possibilities and exceed those client expectations. Since creative control is such a huge motivator and not limited to people who work in what we typically think of as artistic professions—painting, architecture, graphic design—it's of the utmost importance that leaders first equip their teams to act like artists and then stand back and trust them to take it from there. Building relationships is truly an art, not a science; therefore, an inside-out leader must always treat their teams as creative artists.

We had always empowered our real estate development teams to think outside the box. They knew the only expectation we had of them was to wow the customers, which meant they had full creative license to do whatever needed to be done to amaze and delight. This story begins with a prospect along the Washington, DC beltway that wanted to relocate but wouldn't even come out to Columbia to see a building we knew would be perfect for them.

They said, "It's too remote; transportation won't be easy." Feet dragged; excitement was low. We at Manekin knew what a great corridor this area actually was, but how to convince the client? Our team put their heads together and asked, "Where is there a unique opportunity here to catch their attention? What would be the most exciting way for them to turn from prospect into tenant?" "A helicopter," someone said.

If our team wasn't awake to possibility, such an idea might have been laughed at and shot down, and instead, it was applauded. "Why *not* rent a helicopter? Great idea!" was the consensus.

Our team met the prospect at their Washington location and helicoptered them to Columbia to show them the building. From that height, the company could easily take in the road patterns, the proximity to both Baltimore and Washington, and the easy airport access. When they landed and arrived at the building, a sign with their company's name already hung on the building. We wanted to give them the chance to really imagine themselves at home in that location. That's what awakening possibility is all about.

A few months later, they moved in.

## Where Great Ideas Come From

I have learned that this realm of possibility isn't just limited to the leader's imagination, and indeed, it shouldn't be. Inside-out leaders need to bring people together around the table and empower them to speak and lead. Inside-out leaders should focus on awakening others to their own powerful imaginations so they too can see the world anew. After that, leaders throw all ego aside and just listen like crazy (while remembering the importance of note-taking, so no important issue or idea gets forgotten). Because the truth is, success is never a one-person band. One must be smart enough only to know what they don't know.

All the success that Manekin or Seawall accomplished and enjoyed over the years was not due to our own brilliance or great ideas-not at all. Every success came from empowering others as stakeholders and then listening to them. We were simply implementers of other people's great ideas.

This leads us to another key philosophy in an inside-out leadership approach: leaders as conduits.

## Leaders as Conduits

A conduit is, at its most basic definition, a channel through which energy can flow. For inside-out leaders, it is the energy of ideas. Leaders who open themselves with humility to the input of others become vehicles for great ideas to flow through and become reality. The job of inside-out leaders then is to quite literally make other people's dreams come true on a daily basis—to awaken them to possibilities they had never even before imagined and then make them happen.

True leaders are conduits, and to be one, a leader must practice openness and humility. One must be smart enough only to know what they don't know. If we accept that the only real constant in life is change, then we accept the notion that there is always more to learn. Education doesn't end after high school or even after earning three PhDs. Humility allows a leader to be a lifelong learner, to live with their eyes wide open to possibilities, their ears wide open to others, and their hearts wide open to accept the lessons that are ever available all around them.

When leaders surround themselves with mentors and teachers, they are able to mentor and teach others. In this way, good leaders are always empowering new leaders. Everyone has the extraordinary potential to be an inside-out leader. We can all be conduits. A servant-based mentality receives and empowers all who embrace it. It turns the world upside down as we learn to live inside-out.

This is the philosophy, so what about the strategy to put it into practice?

## Listen First, Design After

Since we begin by listening and acting as conduits, there's no need to go into meetings with production designs laid out, planned, and strategized, no need to go in and tell others what's going to happen and how it's going to happen. Acting from the inside-out means always looking to the customer for guidance—in other words, listen first and design after. This strategy is the surest way to exceed expectations every, single, time. Below is one of the best and clearest examples I have of this kind of collaboration with key stakeholders.

## The H.F. Miller Building
## Awakening Possibility in the Neighbors

The Remington neighborhood had already blocked the attempts of two other developers to restore the old Miller manufacturing building. We wondered why the other developers failed. The answer, for the community, was quite straightforward. They wanted to be heard and to be engaged partners in the development of the neighborhood they had grown up in and raised their families in. And we found this desire supremely fair. They would be the ones directly impacted not only by what was built but also by the new people and businesses that moved in. Leaders must not ignore the people directly affected by their products and services, even if those people are not necessarily the end users. For us, the people who lived in the areas under our development needed to be invited in as stakeholders in the process. We didn't want them to merely feel like we were listening; we wanted them to see their fingerprints all over the new developments.

Unfortunately for those two previous developers, much time and money were spent on a strategy that was flawed from the beginning. They had come in, targeted the building, and then *told* the neighbors what was going to happen with the development. They dominated the proceedings instead of acting as conduits. Seawall's strategy was and always has been different. Our inside-out approach allows us to listen first, design after. We had no plan for the Miller Building other than to create great housing for teachers new to Baltimore and collaborative office space for nonprofit organizations focused on public education. We were flexible about how to do this and what else might belong in the building. Just like Manekin's higher purpose had been to be seen as stakeholders in the success of Howard County, so too did Seawall have a vision to be neighbors, not guests, in the Remington community. We had no desire to come in and implement our agenda. The whole overarching vision of Seawall was to be humble servants to those we served. Here in Remington, we didn't want to be one-off developers. The Miller Building would be just the beginning.

And we had to back up our words with actions to prove our extraordinary intentions to the community.

From almost the moment we signed the agreement to purchase the Miller Building, we were hosted by the three community groups. With pen and pad in hand, we shared our vision and then stepped back and took copious notes from those attending the meeting. This was to be as much their building as ours. As our first sign of solidarity and belief in community, we moved our office from downtown Baltimore into the neighborhood so we could sit on people's front stoops. And that's quite literally what we did. Thibault went door, to door meeting the residents, sitting on their stoops, sharing beer, getting to know them, and hearing stories about the neighborhood's rich history. We wanted to learn what they thought would make their community great. We wanted them to know we were more than developers; we were advocates for their community's success. In the spirit of listen first and design after, we hosted brainstorming sessions and brought pizzas. We even served on neighborhood committees to garner ideas from residents, earn their trust, and ultimately, give them the confidence that we were listening and implementing their feedback. Turnout was high for these events, and the participation was key for developing the strategies we used moving forward in development, the strategies that would help us reach success.

Awakening possibility in this disinvested community meant a number of things for these neighbors. First, we awakened the possibility that they could indeed be stakeholders in the process. We were roused by the power of their ideas and showed them the influence of their voice. This by itself was empowering. Beyond that, they awakened to the possibilities for just how the building could be developed. Yes, it was going to be residential units for teachers and office space for nonprofits, but what else? "What if . . ." they mused, "what if there's a coffee shop too? Nothing name brand or franchised, but something small and locally owned? We don't have a coffee shop around here, and that'd be a nice way for us to gather with our growing community and all the new neighbors."

It was such a simple and profound idea, and a beautiful way to bring everyone together under one roof. A freshly brewed cup of coffee is more than a morning pick-me-up; it's a conversation starter, the opportunity to be seen and witnessed, to be regulars—to be in community. In the end, we are all just looking for deeper connections with others.

If the Miller renovation could bring all that with a coffee shop, then we were in. Our brainstorming sessions also awakened the neighbors to the possibilities for just how their community might change down the road, how cleaning up buildings would improve safety, and how the area would be less attractive for drug deals and slumlords. They envisioned young people moving in, baby carriages on the sidewalks again, vibrancy, life.

By awakening this kind of possibility in others, leaders create ripple effects that spread further and wider than their own reach could ever hope to go. By inviting others to be a part of the journey, they may end up surprising you even as you're working to delight them.

## Surprising Ripple Effects

It started with inviting the neighbors to tour the Miller building before development began because we wanted them to experience the full transformation and be a part of the building's journey. Little did we know just how much ownership the neighbors would take in the project. Two doors down in a row house lived Larry, a mild-mannered man always ripe to talk. Larry represents just one example of this ripple effect as he became the Miller's Court building's guardian angel.

As is common on construction sites, materials get hauled in, unloaded, and frequently left overnight, ready to be used the next day-free material with great black-market value for those interested in taking advantage of such things. Late one evening, Larry was sitting on his stoop when he noticed someone prying the plywood off a future window of the Miller building. Without hesitation, he jumped to his feet, yelled at the hooded figure, and chased him down the street until he not only was able to corner him but also to wrestle him to the ground. Another neighbor called the police. They weren't going to let anyone mess with their new building.

Talk about the ripple effect of empowering people to become stakeholders in the vision! Larry put himself in harm's way to protect a project that he wasn't even being paid to be a part of. But he believed in its purpose. When that happens, everyone rows in the same direction and steps up where they can and as needed. It's a beautiful thing to witness.

## Awakening Possibility in the Teachers and Nonprofits

As with the neighbors, we called a round table with teachers and nonprofits to listen to their ideas for how to develop the Miller building. Those in attendance represented our intended audience, and we knew their input would drive the building's progress and function beyond anything we could imagine on our own.

And first, we took them on a tour of the building in her "war-torn" days, still littered with drug paraphernalia and pigeons cooing in the rafters. There was nothing pretty about the tour, but we painted a picture of the possibilities and watched their eyes light up. We shared our vision: create great affordable and supportive housing for teachers new to Baltimore and cost-effective, efficient, and collaborative office space for nonprofits. And, we added—this is a blank canvas. What would you design? The ideas gushed.

Teachers were spending so much time after work at Kinko's making copies of lesson plans at their expense for the following day because the school's equipment was inadequate. Nonprofits (and teachers) were spending a lot of money each month on gym memberships for their own health and self-care. Both groups were completely transparent about how much they could afford in rent. Both stressed the importance of collaboration with like-minded professionals and organizations. Input was direct and specific. We couldn't have asked for more valuable feedback; their ideas were all things we could actionably work to solve.

Designs for the Miller building included a copy center, so teachers could walk down the hall in their robes if they felt like it to prepare for the next day of teaching. A 24-hour fitness center boasted a wealth of equipment and free weights, and even a shower for the nonprofits. An outdoor urban courtyard with grill, fireplace, and Adirondack chairs enticed people for impromptu and planned gatherings. Living rooms within the buildings became great places to hang out.

By listening to our audience, by making them stakeholders in the project, community started to be built even before anyone moved in. On top of that, Seawall was able to implement augmented services like the above that went beyond what's normally expected from both a developer and a landlord because we could design their wants and needs into the very heart of the project.

Our hope was that by giving above and beyond even what our clients could dream up, a ripple would be started. And that ripple would positively affect the students taught by those teachers and the people supported by those nonprofits. Developing the Miller building was never just about creating a shiny new development. Our purpose was built on the hope that by looking out for teachers and nonprofits, they could better look out for those they served. Real estate development for us was and is about creating waves of change within the education sector of Baltimore and the surrounding communities. All we do is bring the skills we have to bear for those with the big ideas and the big hearts who are doing the most important work—educating the next generation.

## The Ripple Continues

Another big piece to the success of the Miller's Court story was that we were only able to meet the clients' rent requirements because of the knowledge we gained from our financing partners, accountants, and lawyers. As stakeholders also in the success of Baltimore communities, these three groups spent hours investing in us and educating us in things like Historic and New Market Tax Credits. They were truly bilingual, able to turn legalese into layman's terms we could follow and learn from. I won't go into detail about how these loans work, but it's basically free money for those renovating historic buildings in distressed neighborhoods. Yes, we also invested thousands of dollars for this consulting, and it was of great value for furthering our visions to the community we were serving, and as you'll see—even beyond our own back doors. We were able to take this knowledge and also build Union Mill in Baltimore and Oxford Mills in Philadelphia in the same spirit as Miller's Court and then go on to build affordable, for-sale, row houses for teachers; as well as develop the food hall, R. House, and Remington Row, which became another hub for invigorating the Remington community.

We also have never believed that this knowledge was ours and ours alone.

We have always hoped that our work in Baltimore and Philadelphia would awaken others to the possibilities for social enterprise within their own cities and that they would be inspired by what we'd been up to. And this hope came true.

The leadership team from the Propel Charter Schools in Pittsburgh was interested in creating affordable teacher housing, similar to what we'd done with Miller's Court, and they had a real vision and a great opportunity for doing so. Just like so many stakeholders had invested in us over the years, offering consultation for free or going above and beyond to help us be successful, so we counted it a great opportunity to give back in the same way. We openly shared with them our inside-out philosophies, and even brought in teachers and nonprofits who lived and worked at Miller's Court to share about their experiences. And we went even beyond that. We wanted to give them all the tools and strategies and as much knowledge as we could to help them replicate our models. Thibault had accumulated a wealth of knowledge regarding the tax credits available in cities to fund developments like these, and more importantly, he'd learned how to translate all the legalese into layman's terms (thanks to the terrific guidance of the attorneys and lawyers he'd worked so closely with over the years of developing in the Baltimore neighborhood). What took Thibault months and months to learn, he was able to pass on in a few hours to the folks from Pittsburgh, helping them kickstart their project with greater confidence and excitement at all the possibilities that lay ahead. Our tenants talked with them about what worked for them and what they appreciated about living at Miller's Court. We didn't charge a consulting fee for this initial visit—this was our gift to them, just as so many others have gifted us with their time and knowledge.

Inside-out leaders don't believe they own their projects.

Certainly, we benefit from them, and certainly so also do the people we serve. Our work in Remington and other Baltimore communities has been transformational, and we think it's something that should be made available to every organization in our city and across the country. Inside-out leaders must always be looking beyond the moment of what they are doing now.

# 8. Exceeding Expectations

Exceeding expectations has become a mindset for everyone working with us. It is how we approach each and every day. Robin Crow shared it succinctly when he said, "There's no straighter road to success than exceeding expectations one day at a time."

It was late at night, and Thibault was at home asleep with his family when the telephone rang.

"Hello?" asked a soft, timid voice on the other end of the receiver.

"Is this Thibault?"

"Yes, this is Thibault. Who's this?"

"It's Joe, one of the residents at Union Mill. I am so sorry to wake you at this hour, but my key fob won't work, and I have to be in class tomorrow at 7:30 a.m." His voice was strained, fatigued.

Thibault's priority was to put him at ease. Thibault told Joe, "I want you to go to the nearest hotel, get a good night's sleep, and we'll have the lock fixed first thing in the morning. Please send me the hotel receipt, and we'll have a check to you by day's end."

A purposeful and genuine company is built on the foundational principle that we will serve our clients to the utmost.

When Joe moved in, he—just like all residents— was given the personal cell phone numbers of everyone responsible for the building just in case any issues arose. We wanted our residents to feel like family and not to hesitate to call these numbers for help. This shining example was not a singular event of how far we would go to embrace our tenants and clients; going above and beyond for those we work with is the heart and soul of our business.

## There's Always More to Give

In the previous chapter, I described what's possible when we awaken others to possibility and listen to their ideas, and I want to impress further this idea that there is still always more we can do and give as leaders. That there are ways to be even more generous, even more thoughtful, and have even more fun trying to find ways to roll out the red carpet for our clients even after a job is finished.

## It's Not What's Typically Done, but It's What Can Be Done

The teachers and nonprofits unleashed a world of possibilities and amenities that would make living at Miller's Court an extraordinary experience for them—copy machines, grills, a gym, and from the neighbors—a coffee shop. That wasn't all we did for them. We wanted to exceed their expectations for us as landlords by becoming stakeholders in their success. The expectation of a landlord is that they will fix your dishwasher when it breaks. As a stakeholder, we could go further. As stakeholders in their success, we put together a "Baltimore in a Box" gift package for each new resident filled with free passes to the movies, restaurants, museums, and a wealth of other places to explore that a new resident might wish to enjoy in their new city. We did this because we wanted them to feel welcomed and connected and excited to live here.

One certainly doesn't expect their landlord to buy them a keg of beer during a winter storm. But that's exactly what we did when a severe snowstorm blanketed Baltimore and canceled school for days on end. The mayor had asked everyone to stay indoors to keep the roads safe. We thought some beer could add some fun to their snow days stuck inside. They could enjoy it in the courtyard or take a pint back up to their apartment.

One doesn't expect their landlord to host a buffet breakfast for them. But four times a year, that's what we do. Bagels, juice, coffee, and muffins, we've got it down by the elevators starting at 6:30 a.m.

There are times we've hosted a dinner with all the teachers in the two buildings and the CEO of the school system. A gathering of novice teachers to break bread with the head of the system and for the CEO to listen to their experiences was a chance to break down traditional walls and forge new connections. The CEO got to listen to her most important constituents, those in the trenches, and learn what's working and what's not, and the teachers got the chance to understand the CEO's vision and higher purpose.

For the nonprofits, we host brown bag lunches a few times a year and bring in people who can help the nonprofits work smarter. And we host a yearly luncheon for all the nonprofits in the building to get together and just enjoy each other's company.

I know I say it often, and it's worth repeating—it's all about relationships.

## Just Doing What We Said We'd Do

My good friend and former colleague at Manekin, David Kinne, used to talk about how other people in the real estate market at the time thought we at Manekin must have been up to something. Why were we getting all the leases? Why were our developments always finished on time? How were we getting approvals and permits so quickly?

As he says, "What we were up to was doing what we said we would do!" This was coming from the man who drove all night to go pick up toilet partitions that hadn't arrived as scheduled. He used his personal vehicle and brought back those partitions so they could be installed and the job completed on the day we promised. So you see, people had a lot of confidence in us because we proved to them time and time again that we would always get it right.

And if we weren't getting it right, or we had a problem, we wouldn't hide it. We'd talk about it. We'd get the county officials involved, permit people, everyone from the start of the design phase straight through to the end. We did whatever it took to show that we would, and that we could satisfy whatever the client's concern was and that we could get the building to function as they wanted or needed. We worked hard to exceed the expectations of every person—employees, contractors, clients, stakeholders, state or city officials, neighbors—everyone, and by doing so, they knew we had their back, and they, in turn, had ours.

Whatever we did, we were partners in it.

## Inside-Out Intention

The journey to get to this place of exceeding expectations comes from intentional, daily efforts. No matter what the situation is in the company—no matter what division, which team, if it involves contractors or clients—the leader must be intentional to always act from the inside-out, furthering the higher purpose rooted in relationships above all else.

There was a short time when I ran the brokerage division at Manekin Corporation. When the economy was going great, the brokers felt like nothing could stop them! But we had a year or so when the economy took a big downturn; it changed everything, and the brokers got scared.

This was the moment for me to really impress upon them just how much of a relationship business—not a transactional business—we were. This was the moment to awaken them to the possibility that the scope of their job was so much greater than they were imagining, that what their typical responsibilities were did not end there, and that this downturn could be an extraordinary opportunity if they shifted their mindset.

The downturn was simply a different phase. During this phase, I told them: Go out and provide your prospects with real estate knowledge and build community with them. Give them more than updates on new developments and the present market for leasing space—give them the kind of information they need to best support their business now. Help them be smarter. Show them you're more than just a transactional commission-driven salesperson; show them you're a stakeholder in their success. Invest in these folks now, so when the economy shifts, and they might be looking to lease space again, well then, maybe they'll think of you. But even if they don't need you as a broker down the road, at least you'll know that your job has meaning because you've served the community and fostered sincere relationships, and that is much more fulfilling than simply earning a commission and getting cut an office check.

Just like the brokers, if leaders are only focused on monetary results like the commission, then we lose the beauty of the journey. The pot of gold at the end of the rainbow is only a function of the journey to get you there.

Implementing all the philosophies and strategies in this book is really quite simple if people are truly passionate about what they do. This daily intention cannot necessarily be taught; rather, it flows from the person inspired by their own strong and personal convictions. That's why intention is tied intimately to higher purpose, because it comes from a mindset. I'd like to think that most of us wake up in the morning and think, "Today, I am going to be extraordinarily intentional!" I'd like to think most wake up and see and act on what's possible. We choose to set a tone for our company, and then we follow through. Of course, it's possible that we need to dig a little deeper within ourselves to find that genuine core, and once we find it—because I promise you it exists—then we can ignite it and live by its light.

Within Seawall Development is a man by the name of Peter DiPrinzio, and he personifies, for me, extraordinary intention fueled by sincere passion. He isn't someone who wakes up with a checklist on his mind of things to accomplish in order to count his day a success but is rather someone who believes so deeply in what he is doing and why he is doing it that he lives from a core place of deep intention that fuels him to go above and beyond the expected, beyond the checklist, beyond the ordinary.

Peter doesn't have a background in real estate—he'd worked with start-ups doing marketing and sales operation. Yet his real passion was food. Before graduating, he'd worked jobs and held internships in the food industry, and after some time in startups, he wanted to get back to being a foodie full-time and to share that passion with his community.

Back when a food hall in Remington was just an idea, Peter approached Seawall about doing a one-day food festival at Miller's Court called the "Remington Chop." His idea was to partner with a few of his friends to bring six chef-led workshops and an all-day beer garden with tacos, oysters, and more to the community. Seawall was all in. "The Chop" sold out of tickets and was a smashing success. After the event, Thibault approached Peter and told him the Remington community had recently been asking Seawall to invest in more food-related projects. We were contemplating a food hall; would he be interested? If passion alone had gotten Peter this far with just the help of his friends, we knew that when given even more resources, time, and trust, he could be an incredible and invaluable addition to the Seawall team, whose new mission was to create a launchpad for chefs.

Peter joined us, and even without a background in development or design, his understanding, knowledge, and passion as a foodie has truly made R. House the transformational development it is today. For months before the launch of the R. House venture, Peter, Thibault, and others from the Seawall team traveled the country visiting dozens of different food courts and talking to the developers and the chefs, asking them, "Now that you've been open three or four years, what did you learn? What would you do differently if you could start over?"

And what the R. House team learned from the developers and chefs, they implemented. The chefs gave them insight into the smallest details that could go a long way in exceeding the expectations of those they worked with and those they served at R. House. They suggested things like high captain's tables with power outlets and just a few tall chairs—some people would sit, some might rather stand. This area of R. House has now become a hub for business meetings and gatherings. Similarly, there are tables designed and built so families can gather, and the children have tables and chairs sized for them. Then there are the details people never see and which support the chefs and the entire operation—like the underground grease trap. The team learned that all chefs have to clean a grease trap, and that it's disgusting, and they hate it. At R. House, we decided to put in a two-gallon grease trap underground that didn't need to be cleaned by hand. It turned out to be both cheaper and easier, and even though the customers don't see or know anything about it, they benefit from it in unseen ways. The chefs don't have to be pulled in ten directions and can instead focus on what they do best—making incredible food.

What has been particularly impressive is how every day, Peter continues to come in with an unmatched enthusiasm and intention to make sure, down to the smallest detail, that the R. House chefs have the vehicle they needed to create great food. He says, as the operations guy, that he is always thinking hard about details. "If we want something to feel a certain way," he explains, "like if we want guests to feel welcome, or if we want the building to feel humble, then I have to consider: how brightly do we shine the lights, what type of music do we play, which chairs should we buy, what colors do we paint with? R. House and the chefs have a vision, so as an operations guy, I come in and say, 'OK, that's our vision. So how do we make that happen every single day for the thousands of people who pass through the food hall?' I put my passion into the little details because they make up the greater whole and create the experience, the *feel* of the place. It's OK to give up control of details too and give control to the tenants working out of the space too because then you know it is going to be right. You have to think through them."

This passion for the details and looking to the customer for their ideas, creates an atmosphere of exceeding expectations that isn't just seen, but actually felt and personally experienced by the customers.

They are leaders who think from the inside-out.

# Section Four

*Leaving a Legacy*

# 9. Living Legacies

The optimal result of leaving legacies is the ripple effect it has not only on the present moment but for generations to come. A stone thrown in a pond creates a ripple; it begins at the center of the impact and grows larger and larger as the ripple spreads out further and further. A leader helps orchestrate one event centered on relationships to produce results, and that one event produces more results, and those results produce even more results. The stories that follow about leaving living legacies demonstrate actions, stones thrown, that have rippled out to have personal and professional effects far beyond their opening motif.

Years ago, my wife Brigitte was a master's degree student at, what at that time was, TAI Sophia. The university and Brigitte's passion were teaching, learning, and advancing the holistic approach to health and wellness. Brigitte shared this story with me, which has become the heart and soul of leaving a legacy and its ripple effect.

> Many centuries ago, an architect came to the people of Heidelberg and rolled out his parchments of drawings. "Good people," he said, "You asked me to design a grand cathedral. Here it is."
>
> The townspeople gathered around the table as the architect shared his vision for the building and described its structure. "This is the foundation, the basis for everything else that's built. It will take one hundred years to properly finish it.
>
> The townspeople began counting on their fingers. "Why,

that's our lives, plus our children's lives, plus our grandchildren's lives." A murmur spread through the crowd.

The architect pointed to a new section: "Then the walls will be built. They're fairly easy; it should only take fifty years to complete." Emma, one of the few citizens who could count above ten without taking her shoes off, declared, "It will take the entire lives of our great-grandchildren to finish those walls."

The architect shifted the papers uneasily but continued. "Then there is the roof; that's the real problem. It will take 250 to 350 years to finish.

After a few minutes, Emma announced: "We can finish the new cathedral in the lives of our great-great-great-great-great-great-great-great grandchildren."

A stunned silence blanketed the room.

Finally, a voice in the back spoke and said: "So, when do we start?"

This story is a powerful tale about how what we invest in and envision today may take years to get rooted, its potential not fully realized for generations to come. I'm humbled, quite frankly, by the people who have gone before and set the example for me and others to follow. The people who demonstrated, through their daily and intentional efforts, that leadership means looking beyond the present and beyond the fulfillment of one's own needs. The ones who said, What's possible? The ones who lived knowing the decisions they made then had the potential to affect generations to come. The ones who had the courage to take responsibility for those future generations by dreaming big and taking action, even if they, in some cases, were never to see those dreams take root or bear fruit.

So often, we think of leaving a legacy as something that is offered after we die, usually a monetary gift, an endowment to a university or nonprofit, for example. Personally, I, like others, think legacies are best left during one's lifetime where the results can be seen, felt, and shared. It takes more effort and energy, and we may only be able to envision the fruit of the seeds we plant, and still, it's important to plant them.

At one time in my life, I had the opportunity to serve on the board of TAI Sophia. The institute was founded by husband-and-wife team Bob Duggan and Dianne Conolly and became the first acupuncture school in the US to receive accreditation. Bob and Dianne's vision for the legacy they wanted to leave became an inspiring reminder for me to thoughtfully consider how all my present actions might affect future generations. They became key influencers in integrative medicine and paved the way for students and patients to look deeply into themselves for the answers to their health and well-being. Over the decades, hundreds—perhaps thousands—have graduated from their programs. Those hundreds have gone on to touch the lives of hundreds more. In this way, it isn't just the direct graduates who experience the impact of TAI Sophia. As graduates are themselves transformed, thousands of others also benefit from the transformation.

Bob and Dianne posed these questions at the start of nearly every conference or meeting I attended of theirs: "It remains each of our responsibility, as we go along our way of living, to always consider two things. One, in everything we think, say, and do, are we honoring those who came before us? And two, are we serving our children's children's children?" I have never forgotten their words, and I find them much better questions than the one so often posited, which is: What do I want to do?

That question is far too small. The bigger question is: How will I serve?

To be a living legacy requires passionately taking responsibility for our unique gifts and actively sharing and using them for the good of others. In this way, they will have a life beyond that of their own because we will be serving a cause greater than our own. Leaders serve the lives of people they may never meet by bringing their skills and talents to bear now.

## Socially Responsible Leadership

Max De Pree, author of four books on leadership, shared that "the first responsibility of a leader is to define reality and the last is to say thank you. In between the two, the leader must become a servant and debtor." Servant leaders share inherent and essential characteristics, as outlined in Robert Greenleaf's book titled simply, *Servant Leadership*. These characteristics are listening, empathy, healing, awareness, persuasion, conceptualization, foresight, stewardship, commitment, and *building community*.

The first three pillars of my life have always been these: my wife Brigitte, our children (and now our children's children), and the business. My fourth pillar is community, and—although I grew up witnessing my dad's engagement in the community and how much it meant to him—I didn't think to integrate this fourth pillar into my life until I was ten years into my career. Its importance became clear to me after I had been offered an opportunity to be a part of the Leadership Howard County program. For over ten years, the county was my home away from home. Living in Baltimore and driving to Columbia each day, I thought, through my narrow lens, that Howard County was in Columbia—not the other way around. The borders of my business life were roughly two square miles outlined neatly between two major highways. And outside those boundaries, I could only spread my wings far enough to get to the county seat in Ellicott City to file and pick up permits.

The leadership program expanded my view of the county, which expanded my view of our company and the larger role we could play.

For one year, each month, our group explored a different facet of Howard County like: healthcare, the arts and entertainment, education, etc. There were things happening in the county that I had previously known nothing about, and by connecting with the people and organizations who would never have otherwise crossed my path, we were, together, able to leverage our new professional and personal relationships for the benefit of all. And our company could become more effective at making a difference in the lives of the people in Howard County.

Later, I was asked to join the inaugural class of Leadership Maryland, which was similar but on a larger scale. There, I learned how we could see Howard County under the umbrella of the state of Maryland and how our county could affect all other counties and vice versa. The leadership programs changed my leadership perspective. From then on and every day after, I woke up with the same intention: What role could we take as a company and I as an individual representing the company to be of value to a larger community? While real estate development has always been inextricably linked to the fate of the community in which it occurs, our developments weren't about just building another great building and exceeding the expectations of our clients. Real estate, for us, became about serving the community in ways that the positive impact of our involvement could be felt at the moment and for generations to come. Inside-out leadership always takes into account its effect on not only the people living today but also the people who will live tomorrow. Leaders may never see the final result of any of their work, but the fact remains that someone has to put the shovel in the ground and think about what can happen.

We must all stay cognizant that every visible action we take leaves an impression. We must always be thinking about these impressions and choosing the most socially responsible route. No matter the industry, every company and each individual can ask: How can we/I create improvements while still respecting the culture, character, and needs of the communities we serve?

Many servant-leaders have crossed my path and influenced my personal journey over the years as they demonstrated socially responsible, forward-thinking, and compassionate legacy building in everything they touched. One of these leaders who touched many deeply was Walter Sondheim, a man whose gifts shaped the very city of Baltimore and the lives of so many of her citizens. His resume could be a book in itself. Walter was the Chairman of the Baltimore Housing Authority, the Director of Baltimore Urban League, the Chairman of the Charles Center of Inner Harbor Management, and President of the Baltimore City School Board.

Two particular stories from Walter's life stand out to me as examples of legacy building and working to better the future.

The first is that Walter, as Chairman of the Housing Authority, was singularly responsible for creating the legislation that tore down the high-rise, low-income housing in Baltimore. He talked about what Section 8 buildings symbolized, saying, "When you drive by those buildings, you know who lives there and why. And if you live there, you know why too." He wanted to obliterate the stigmas and the segregation those buildings created and represented. The buildings came down, and, in their place, projects like Lexington Terrace were developed for mixed-income residents. There was no differentiation in the houses that were built—all were equal.

The second story is this. In 1954, the landmark Supreme Court Case, *Brown v. Board of Education*, ruled that racial segregation of children in public schools was unconstitutional. Walter was the chairman of the school board at the time and he didn't waste a minute. "We're going to desegregate the Baltimore Schools," he said. And they did, at a time and in a place where things were extremely segregated. Walter might not be proud to see just how segregated the schools in Baltimore are again in practice, but what he did made an impression and a difference. His no-nonsense, say it like it is, stance on issues of social and racial justice made a mark on the youth who would become the city's future leaders. Those youth are now grown, and they continue in his work, making great strides to bring equity to our city.

This leads me to another servant-leader from Baltimore, who is also connected to Walter Sondheim's legacy even as he has built his own. Joseph T. Jones is the founder and CEO of The Center for Urban Families (CFUF) of Baltimore, a nonprofit "service organization established to empower low-income families by enhancing both the ability of women and men to contribute to their families as wage earners and of men to fulfill their roles as fathers." Jones has received innumerable awards and honors for his leadership and one of them happens to be the Walter Sondheim Public Service Award presented by the Greater Baltimore Committee, to honor the memory of Walter, which serves to highlight the far-reaching impact of legacies.

Joe Jones grew up on the streets hustling drugs, being incarcerated, and witnessing how important the relationship of fathers to families is for a child's well-being—and the parent's well-being, whether they are in a relationship or not. He founded CFUF to do three things: reconnect dads to families, allow the under-employed or unemployed to find meaningful work after going through job training, and to help young couples new to parenthood learn how to be a family.

The nonprofit's work reminds me again of the Patch Adams movie and the four fingers scene that I mentioned in the introduction. Each person who comes to the center learns to see beyond, to act beyond their problems, and see what's possible. The families who have been reconnected, the couples learning life skills, and the formerly unemployed/underemployed have learned the skills necessary to be successful in employment and in their personal lives. As a result, they will show their children the road worth traveling. Their children will see their parents as role models for their future.

This nonprofit not only impacts the families it serves, but the programming is also now recognized nationwide and is used in policy development, workforce development, and civic engagement. The good work, the living legacy—started by Joe and implemented by those serving now ripples throughout the nation and across generations.

Leaders of this caliber humble and inspire my journey because they have fully immersed themselves in the amazing possibilities of what their work could accomplish. In them, I see the extraordinary intention we all have inside us. It's something we can develop further if we are willing to witness others, learn from them, and imagine new possibilities for inside-out leadership. By watching those we admire, our own thinking and leadership style is transformed.

With leaders like these always on my mind and a tug to return to the education sector in hopes of using my talents to make a greater impact, I made a pivotal career move back in 2000 when I decided to retire from the family real estate company in order to pursue that call.

## Crafting Legacies

I wanted to take the skill sets I had acquired over my twenty-five years in real estate and apply them to the next generation of learners who would become citizens and leaders in their communities. Real estate had helped me sharpen my leadership skills, but deep down I knew it was only a vehicle to what I believed was my purpose. Education was my calling. I'd always believed in the importance of public education. It was a learning platform for students and also an economic engine that could change the trajectory for students, their families, and their cities.

My first opportunity to dive back into education came with the opportunity to form, with friends, The Foundation for Rural Education in Maryland, an organization to support schoolteachers with mini-grants in the rural counties of the western part of the state, that would enable teachers to provide better learning opportunities for their students.

The idea for the foundation came from a longtime friend and mentor of mine, Chuck Callanan, who, after leading a private school in Baltimore for ten years, relocated to Maine and began traveling through rural subdivisions. He discovered that schoolteachers desperately needed more financial support; something I would later discover was also true in rural Maryland as I met and listened to superintendents, principals, and classroom teachers in Allegany and Garrett County. District-wide pizza sales and raffles weren't enough. Schools needed additional resources to support student learning opportunities, but there were no large foundations to create a stable base of support for them. Their needs were urgent and real. Using the same model Chuck set up when he created the Trout Foundation in Maine, a group of friends and I used his methods to create a similar foundation in Maryland. Twice a year, we reviewed grant applications and funded them quickly—within thirty days—so teachers could feel an immediate, positive impact.

These funds were often used to provide opportunities to take students outside their rural surroundings for the first time, like getting to visit the Chesapeake Bay and study its tributaries to truly understand its influence on their mountainous community. By getting outside the classroom and experiencing their world firsthand, not only do test questions become more meaningful and relevant to their lives, but they also gain new perspectives that empower their own learning process. It's easy to see what the potential for teachers and students is when foundations like these are formed. Foundations are a great way to leave living legacies; you often get to "see" and enjoy the fruits of your labor now, knowing the effects will continue to ripple as those children grow.

There is also a deeper legacy embedded within this story, and that is the life of Chuck Callahan.

I'd met Chuck in my late teen years, a few years before I even entered my father's real estate business. I fondly remember sitting with him, and his wife and child, on their deck, drinking coffee and munching his homemade oatmeal bread after our 6 a.m. runs on the beach. Chuck became an incredible mentor to me over the years. Though he had started out leading the construction business his father started, he ended up earning his master's degree in English and teaching in a high school for years, before leading an independent school in Baltimore and finally, forming The Trout Foundation. I always admired his dedication to education and the knowledge he had of how to best serve principals, teachers, and students.

Chuck followed his path, doing what he felt called to do. Did he ever expect that someone else would come along and replicate his methods? Probably not. He was thinking about having a greater impact on the rural communities of Maine, and yet, his passion, insights, and ideas were to be carried throughout rural Maryland as well. As leaders follow their calling, they open up doors for others to follow theirs, and that momentum just keeps going. Chuck invested in relationships his entire life; he truly embodies an inside-out leader who always thought outside the box. He invested in me when I wasn't on a clear path, and yet somehow, years down the road, I was able to take his success and replicate it—something I never dreamed was possible when I was young and in my twenties and munching on homemade oatmeal bread. Chuck's legacy took on a life of its own and traveled even further than he had ever imagined. This is the beauty of leaving legacies.

Inside-out leaders truly hope that if they've created something successful and meaningful, that others will be inspired to take their work or ideas even further.

And now to return to my own path after retirement from the family business because things didn't end with The Foundation for Rural Education in Maryland. They were just beginning. Soon after launching the foundation, I got what was for me, a true opportunity of a lifetime. I find it incredible that when we set a purpose, sometimes opportunities just come to us that we never knew existed. Doors open to make a larger impact on a community just because we have grounded ourselves in an extraordinary intention to leave a valuable and positive impression.

My exciting opportunity came one summer while our family was on vacation. The phone rang, and it was Bill Struever, a legendary urban developer I knew in Baltimore. He was also a school system commissioner. He began in an uncharacteristic matter-of-fact tone: "Look, Donald. There's been a recent opening in the school system for an interim chief operating officer. This person is responsible for overseeing the non-academic side of public education." OK, I thought, as he continued on. Although he started the conversation with calm and calculated opening lines, his intensity, passion, and resolve about the position soon became evident. Knowing Bill all too well, I could see him pacing around his office with his arms moving like an orchestra conductor, spouting off the importance of shaking up an old and well-established bureaucracy. "What it needs is someone from the business community who can bring new thinking and action!" he went on and on. Lost in the visuals of Bill's tone, I realized that I was exhausted just listening to him. When he did pause, out of breath, I wasn't sure if he was asking for me to help him find someone to fill the position or whether he wanted me to take on the role, so I just waited for him to continue.

"Well?" he finally said, "are you interested?"

Was I interested? The offer was daunting. Our family business operated on a budget of $11 million; the school district's budget was $850 million! I wondered if the inside-out approach to business and leadership was transferable. My leadership style emphasizes active engagement and seeking direction from those working within the system. Sure, it worked in the classroom and with a real estate team of about thirty people, but could I empower hundreds of employees with the same skill sets that had served me all those years? Could I help them feel like they were making a difference every single day? Would the stakeholders who supported me in the past continue to be a resource moving forward? The answer, I would learn later, was "Yes! But the uncertainties swirled in my head, leaving me speechless. I asked Bill for some time to think about it. He said, of course.

I consulted with my wife and kids and sought guidance from none other than Walter Sondheim, the grandfather of so many of Baltimore's successes. He told me the opportunities I would have as the interim chief operating officer were critically important to the economic development of Baltimore. He told me that public education was like a production line creating the next generation of citizens and leaders. He spoke to the higher purpose, the reason beyond the day-to-day duties the job entailed, and told me to center my vision on how the position would affect students, teachers, and principals for generations to come. These insights shaped my decision to accept the position.

Of one thing I was certain—the position was not for the faint of heart. It would be overwhelming and challenging, a twenty-four-hour-a-day, seven days a week kind of commitment, and it would also afford me the opportunity to make an even bigger impact—something I'd always hoped to do. With the blessing of my family, I called Bill back and accepted this new journey with open arms.

Is being involved in projects like these what it means to leave a legacy? At that point in my life, I could be out doing something just for me. But that wouldn't satisfy my drive to be engaged in the effort, engaged with the enterprises doing the work that changes the direction of our communities for years to come. Today, the work we do in the Baltimore City Schools, how we define what public education looks like and how to fund it, is building a foundation for a future that I may never see. I may or may not be around to appreciate that incoming three-year-old graduating from high school ready for a post-secondary education fifteen years from now. But I believe in that little three-year-old, and I don't need to enjoy the fruit of their success to believe that waking up each morning, with the intention to make only those decisions that will serve them down the road, is the absolute best thing I can do. Our work as leaders is, without a doubt, most meaningful and impactful when shared freely with the next generation. We have the chance to multiply our impact by scaling what we've learned to the generations that come after us.

When we choose to leave living legacies, we must remember: It's not just us. We do that great work alongside others also engaged in the effort of bringing our unique qualities to bear on the future of our children's children's children. The possibilities are endless. Since inside-out leadership is rooted in looking beyond our own front doors, it can be said that we wouldn't be inside-out leaders if we didn't give the same effort to others and to the community as we give to our own company. By finding ways to partner in the community, whether on boards or on commissions, we can find ways to get more than twenty-four hours out of our day while being cognizant about the work-life balance. We can offer our time and expertise to help open up doors that community organizations might never be able to open on their own. As leaders, our expertise, be it marketing operations, strategic planning, or financing is worth its weight in gold to those looking for guidance.

Leaders get to be enablers of the growth and success of the organizations they partner with and offer their skill sets to.

And as you can see, legacies come in all shapes and sizes. Building a cathedral is a pretty large legacy and picking up trash is a relatively small one. And yet both can have huge effects. Both have the potential to impact millions through the momentum of the ripple effect. Both are about offering our talents, our time, our strengths, our passion, and our very lives as gifts to others in any way we are able.

Not long ago, Brigitte and I took one of our grandchildren to volunteer during a Hot Lunch program at Paul's Place, a nonprofit in Baltimore. Our grandson's responsibility was to serve the water while others served food. He was about eight years old and took his role very seriously. His commitment to filling and refilling glasses, so those community members could finish their lunches, was his gift to them.

That, to my Brigitte and me, counts as legacy just as much as forming a foundation and serving on community boards.

I believe as we move through our lives we must stop every once in a while, to look back with open arms and ask, "For as long as I have been here, have I done all I wanted to accomplish personally and professionally? Have I missed even a single opportunity to do my best? Or do I wake up every day and say I tried my best to make a difference in the world around me?" And if after this little thought experiment, I have answered truthfully that I really am doing my best, then I know I am on the right track.

# 10. Bearing Witness

The earliest memory I have of my father is seeing him on the tiny screen of our brown box TV. It was 7:00 a.m. on a Sunday morning, and he was on one of those early morning programs that few actually watch on a Sunday. My father was speaking with the leaders of the Children's Guild, a preschool program for children with emotional learning disabilities; he was discussing the importance of the work they were doing and their outcomes. Other early memories are waking up, again on Sunday mornings, to find my father hosting meetings around the long table in our living room with gentlemen from the synagogue to make sure it was running as a successful community. Sure, it was special to see him on the TV and hosting those important discussions, yet at that time in my life, I was hoping to have my dad at home and available to us kids. I didn't fully understand the motivation and intention behind his actions or the legacy he was leaving. Later in his life, my father was interviewed about Manekin Corporation and said, "Baltimore City has been incredibly giving to our ability to run a successful business. I have a responsibility to give back to Baltimore, so it can be a successful city as well." From as far back as my memory goes, my father has always been a role model to me for what being a connected, involved, and generous citizen means. As a child, I bore witness to his example and took his actions and way of being with others to heart.

My father's example in my life has inspired my thoughts on the subject of legacy twofold. First, we consider who it is that is witnessing our actions and what effect our actions might have on their lives and the lives of the people they touch for generations to come. And second, a defining characteristic of inside-out or servant leadership is to consider ways that we, ourselves, bear witness to others every day—how we honor the lives of the people we meet and honor the communities in which we live. In this way, I believe legacies can truly be left every day of the week. Often, these two standpoints happen simultaneously.

We can be role models while honoring our communities at the same time.

## Bearing Witness to the Talent and Needs of Others

One way that Seawall bears witness to the community is through the launch of what they call The Remington Storefront Challenge. Seawall recognizes the great talent and diversity of Baltimore and also recognizes that there are many barriers to entry for new entrepreneurs looking to have a brick-and-mortar location. Under the leadership of David Goldman, the team put their heads together to ask, how can we give the people with the great ideas an opportunity to make their ideas happen? How can we be a launchpad for these entrepreneurs who may be operating out of a basement or at maker and farmers markets to establish a base, a following, and discover who they are as a company?

A big barrier for young startups is most often capital. Another is finding a good location for their audience, and other barriers include things like being a woman or a minority. The Remington Storefront Challenge seeks to remove those barriers, so people can focus on what they do best while also garnering support from stakeholders to help them meet their business goals.

The Remington Storefront Challenge awards, on a rotating basis, two pop-up retail locations to two applicants for 12-24 months in the heart of Remington, completely rent-free. The winners are chosen by a panel of Remington residents, anchor institutions, and local business owners. In this way, the Remington community as a whole, along with Seawall and all their stakeholders, gets to bear witness to the budding talents in Baltimore and provide opportunities that have the potential to reach far beyond this present moment while meeting the needs of today.

Another example of leaving legacies every day of the week comes in the form of this simple story. While out on a walk with my grandchildren one day, I stopped to pick up a bottle and put it in a nearby trash can. "Gramps," one of the children said, "that's what my dad does."

I had modeled a behavior long ago that my son, their father, picked up, and now they bear witness to two generations of family members modeling a behavior that they will undoubtedly remember and repeat going forward. This is a true legacy indeed.

We can think of legacies as teaching moments that last a lifetime. We ask ourselves: Will the recipient of the action gain from this experience? Will they capture it for themselves and one day demonstrate it for others? The hope that they will gain from it spurs us on, and we continue to walk the path of leaving living legacies, never imposing, but rather offering our experiences to others to be interpreted as they deem fit and to use for their own higher purposes.

## Being Role Models Others Might Witness

Integrating inside-out beliefs into one's life often starts with witnessing the philosophies in action, like the following story from a weekend morning I spent with two of our grandchildren. Celebrating the unsung hero is an integral value in my own life and one I hope to spread to others so the ripple of deep-rooted appreciation can spread further and further and be felt by many, many more people than just those whose lives I am able to personally touch.

The sun rose bright and beautiful that Saturday, and I was glad to be spending the morning with two of our grandchildren. We often went to their favorite breakfast joint and then went to see the construction efforts at Remington Row, which was just nearing completion. We often went to the site because I wanted them to witness all that had been accomplished from month to month. With the sun now high in the sky, we sought the cool shade of an elm tree and watched the workers painting signage on the exterior wall. It was precarious work up there on the scaffolding. Through the windows, carpenters and laborers put finishing touches on offices and apartments. Their dedication to making the project completion deadline struck me deeply, and I was in awe of them. Even if they were being paid overtime to work on the weekend, they were my heroes. I genuinely looked up to them and their commitment to their work. While my grandchildren and I relaxed on a bench, the laborers—and countless others around the city—were doing the field work that kept projects on schedule. Most staff at Seawall worked daily in a comfortable office, but the team of contractors in front of me worked through the winter without heat and the summer without air conditioning. If a roof was not on a building yet, then they even worked through rain while standing in puddles with their electric tools. Turning to my grandchildren, I asked them to come closer.

"Watch carefully those that are working. Just as we're hanging out together, those working here could be with their children on this beautiful Saturday or maybe just sleeping in, hoping to catch up on some rest after a long week of work. They were asked to work on this Saturday—and many other Saturdays—because they knew their company had made a commitment to meet a deadline so the new residents could move in as promised. They should be celebrated for all they have contributed. Maybe what we should do together is shout a big thanks to those on the scaffolding and then enter the building and personally visit each person working and give them a high five."

As I spoke, my grandchildren's expressions changed from just interested to inspired as they watched these hard-working men and women through new eyes. They were building the structures that would become residences, offices, and retail spaces. Our grandchildren enthusiastically agreed with the idea to personally congratulate and celebrate the workers, whispering excitedly with each other about how they could create delight for these heroes.

My heart felt truly fulfilled when I witnessed this lesson sink into their minds at such an early age and saw the smiles on the worker's faces as they exchanged high-fives with my grandchildren, complete with giggles and laughs.

**Immediate and Everlasting Legacies**

Before Thibault asked to start Seawall Development with me, he had been working internationally in a program called Playing for Peace (now

Peace Players International). I share his story because I find the legacy impact of the Peace Players model both immediate and everlasting.

Thibault had a number of global experiences after graduating from college, including two years working with the United Way, that fueled his passion for changing the world and influenced his thinking on how he wanted to be involved; namely, that he didn't want to create incremental change-he wanted to create a movement. After reconnecting with a college friend, Sean Tuohey, who'd been living in Ireland playing pro basketball, Thibault saw a way forward. Sean had born witness to the division that continued to exist in Ireland between Catholics and Protestants and wanted to do something to bridge the divide. He imagined children coming together across religious divides and finding common ground through the sport of basketball. He wanted to awaken others to the possibility that children could unite through sports and then envision and create a more peaceful world together.

After launching the program in Ireland, Sean invited Thibault to join their efforts as they launched the program next in South Africa. Despite Nelson Mandela's efforts, the separation between blacks and whites remained starkly evident, and HIV continued to spread through the black population affecting families in ways unimaginable. There was a groundswell of efforts prompted by Mandela to bridge the generational isolation that still existed and find ways to educate children about the dreaded disease, so they could become the generation that would affect its decline.

The essence of the Playing for Peace program was to use the sport of basketball, new to South Africa, as a way to not only bring the racially divided segments of the population together but to also have time and opportunity to educate the young players about disease and the benefits of healthy lifestyles. Sean and Thibault spent long days meeting with schools throughout Durban, South Africa, sharing the vision and garnering support for this effort. Coaches were not flown in from outside but recruited from the townships as the Playing for Peace leadership fully understood that those living there would be the most credible and influential coaches, teachers, and mentors.

Success was immediate, dramatic, and felt throughout Durban. The immediate return was that the children of Durban finally had the opportunity to see each other as they are and understand what they share in common and how they differ. The children of the private schools with their Nike shoes would shoot hoops with children from the townships wearing no shoes at all. Teams were built not as one school against another but integrated. The vision was coming to fruition as the coaches, teachers, mentors, and youth started to see the divides that had existed for generations begin to dissolve. Children experienced deeper and authentic connections as they understood more of each other through sports and teams, and they were receiving health education that they never had before.

The Peace Players legacy is far-reaching both in the sense of bridging divides and in terms of the health and welfare of families for generations to come. The program now extends to multiple countries, including Israel, Cyprus, and the US. A core part of the program is bringing coaches—who are highly skilled in conflict transformation and leadership development—to be role models and examples to the youth. The youth bear witness to healthy communication and behaviors and get to take those traits on for themselves.

Furthermore, the leaders within the organization and out in the field get to bear witness, during their lifetime, to young people from diverse communities who have experienced racial conflict, coming together in friendship, learning to see themselves as positively connected to those around them, and transforming their communities together through the simple act of uniting in understanding and empathy.

The leaders get to bear witness to the incredible things happening in the lives of those youth, and so, it becomes their responsibility to share the stories and to help keep the momentum going.

# An Epilogue:
# Where to From Here

I knew at some point that my sharing would end, and I wasn't sure what title it should have. It was in my mind not to label the closure Conclusion or Final Thoughts. Both appeared as an end, and I wanted it to be more about where it could be taken. As I shared at the beginning, I am hopeful that you take from this what you wish. Keep what resonates and toss what doesn't. Writing this book was a natural next step for me wishing to bear witness to the great people who have inspired me with their philosophies, ideas, support, and guidance by sharing them with you.

My father, who was my greatest source of inspiration for how to live an inside-out life, took me on a drive once when I was just twenty-two years old. It was the summer of my internship at Manekin Corporation. "Donald," he asked, "Have I ever taken you to see the neighborhood where I grew up?" "No, I don't believe so," I said, my ears perking up to hear his story. We drove to West Baltimore and turned on Ruxton Avenue. Like many of Baltimore's neighborhoods, row houses filled the street. My dad pulled over, put the car in park, and pointed at the end unit that he called home. I knew my father was one of five children, born and raised in Baltimore by my grandparents who had immigrated from Russia at the end of the nineteenth century; and I knew some other snippets of stories he'd shared, but the reality of their lives didn't hit home for me until that moment.

Dad took a deep breath: "Our family was poor as church mice. Five kids shared two bedrooms, boys in one, girls in the other. I shared a bed with one of my brothers. Did you know that my father—your grandfather—owned a small grocery on the other side of town? My mother used to take the trolley blocks across town each and every day to bring him his lunch and dinner, and sometimes she couldn't make it, so I would make the delivery. If it was a rainy day, my father would close the store long enough to stand out in the middle of the street to make sure the trolley stopped for me. Dad always thought my older brother and I would follow in his footsteps. Until after the war, that is." He paused and smiled, a glow in his eye as the memories came flowing back. "We both served in WWII, and when the war ended, and we went home, it just seemed like there was more we wanted to do to invest in our community. I only had a high school diploma, and my brother had a law degree, back in those days, you could receive a law degree while obtaining an undergraduate degree. We decided to hang out our shingle as a residential real estate company. Well, we soon learned that this kept us away from our families at nights and on weekends. We decided to switch gears and go into commercial real estate instead. It's been an incredible journey for us, and now—maybe—for you too."

With a warm glow, he told me tales of all the stakeholders that supported him and his brother as the company grew, about the amazing team of people that worked with them, and of the success they'd experienced while they maintained their firm commitment to their community. Many years down the road, I wanted my father to write down these stories as a way to share the lessons with future generations. He was only able to write two pages though before he passed away. His stories transformed and shaped my life. His legacy lives on through me, and perhaps his inside-out life finds new breath within these pages and within your heart as well.

The four major paths: Creating a Purposeful Company, Building Relationships, Awakening Possibility, and Leaving Legacies, and all the thoughts that fell within were guiding forces for me, passed down from my father and many other great mentors, and I hope they will be for you as well. Building relationships, placing your purpose before your methods and functionalities, empowering others, seeing beyond problems to solutions, listening first then implementing, leading from the first-person plural, shining the spotlight on and celebrating all the musicians like a conductor, and of course, exceeding all expectations—these are the heart and soul of inside-out leadership.

I hope for you that at some time, you will sit in an "Adirondack chair," mug in hand, and watch your children and grandchildren, glowing to yourself as the recollections of those preceding years come to the surface. It's for them that you lived this life, and it's also for them that you continue to dream of the ways they will create their own kind of future where they too can sit back and bask in the warm glow of all they have accomplished.

As I remove "pen from hand," I am reminded of two wonderful lines in the book titled Walking with Grandfather by Joseph Marshall III, where he shares that, "The tracks we leave on the land will disappear over time. The tracks we leave in the hearts and minds of others will never fade."

The important thing is to show up each day ready to serve and then go from there.

# Acknowledgments

As I have shared throughout this book, so much of the road traveled has been because of those that mentored, guided, and worked with me—some still present and some no longer with us. They are prominently acknowledged throughout the book by their teachings.

To Asha Myers who gave this writing a soul. Asha never lost sight of what I wanted to communicate. Her ability to take my words and bring them to a higher life is felt throughout the pages.

A special thanks go to members of Manekin Corporation who voiced their recollections, read these words, and provided their thoughts.

To the Loyola University Maryland and University of Baltimore MBA students who took the time to give their insights into this writing and share their beliefs.

To those at Seawall, whose work has been captured within these pages about the road traveled, you have each deeply impacted me with how you so embody inside-out leadership and far exceeding expectations.

To Randy Gerwig, who captured the essence of inside-out leadership by articulating the importance of celebrating the unsung heroes and paying homage to those—who day in and day out—do the work that produces the outcomes imagined.

To Ben Allen, who has orchestrated much of this writing by providing his insights, direction, and talent to make this book happen.

To our son Thibault, who had the vision to build a company of purpose where real estate brings community together.

And saving the best for last—my wife Brigitte, who has stood by me for all these years and has given so much to our children, helping them rise to be who they are today.

# Resources

**Books:**

*Leadership Is an Art* by Max DePree
*Leadership Jazz* by Max DePree
*David and Goliath* by Malcolm Gladwell
*Servant Leadership* by Robert Greenleaf
*Larger Than Yourself* by Thibault Manekin
*Walking with Grandfather: The Wisdom of Lakota Elders* by Joseph M. Marshall III
*Better Places, Better Lives: A Biography of James Rouse* by Joshua Olsen
*In Search of Excellence: Lessons from America's Best Run Companies* by Tom Peters and Robert Waterman
*Start with Why* by Simon Sinek

**Articles:**

"After the Sale Is Over" Theodore Levitt, Harvard Business Review
"Marketing Success Through Differentiation-of Anything" Theodore Levitt, Harvard Business Review
"Creating a Purpose-Driven Organization" Robert E. Quinn and Anjan V. Thakor, Harvard Business Review
"Crafting Strategy" Henry Mintzberg, Harvard Business Review
"Why Ford Hired a Furniture Maker as CEO" Jerry Useem, The Atlantic
"The Best Bosses Are Humble Bosses" Sue Shellenbarger, Wall Street Journal

**Videos:**

*How Great Leaders Inspire Action* Simon Sinek
*Revisionist History: My Little Hundred Million* Malcolm Gladwell (Podcast)

# About the Authors

**Donald Manekin** has worked on community-focused real estate development, civic leadership and philanthropic missions in the Baltimore-Washington region for more than four decades. He learned the real estate business from his father, Harold Manekin, co-founder of the Manekin Corporation. Donald opened the company's first satellite office in fast-growing Howard County in 1979. At Donald's direction as partner and senior vice president of Manekin, the company developed a team-oriented approach to real estate development.

Upon retiring from Manekin in 2000, Donald served as chief operating officer of the Baltimore City Schools for two years; he managed an $850 million budget, streamlined its financial systems, and oversaw its blueprint for high school reform.

Donald has served as the regional president of the National Association of Industrial and Office Properties and was a member of its national board. He has taught graduate students at Johns Hopkins University, M.I.T., and Loyola University-Maryland and has served on a number of boards, including: United Way of Central Maryland, Leadership Howard County, Columbia Foundation, Teach for America, and Open Society Institute-Baltimore.

In 2006, Donald and his son, Thibault, founded Seawall Development Company. Seawall believes in re-imagining the real estate development industry so that the built environment empowers communities, unites our cities, and helps launch powerful ideas.

He can be reached at dmanekin@seawall.com

**Asha Myers** is a freelance ghostwriter and book editor, specializing in nonfiction and memoir. In her background in human development, social work, and nonprofit management, where she worked one-on-one with at-risk youth and families, helping them share their stories and rewrite their narratives as a way to empower their voice and regain a sense of agency.

She works with authors whose stories hold truths about how to transform our global human community by first transforming one's own heart, mind, and soul.

Asha lives in the beautiful Driftless region of Wisconsin with her husband and daughter.

She can be reached at asha@junebabystudio.com

Apprentice House is the country's only campus-based, student-staffed book publishing company. Directed by professors and industry professionals, it is a nonprofit activity of the Communication Department at Loyola University Maryland.

Using state-of-the-art technology and an experiential learning model of education, Apprentice House publishes books in untraditional ways. This dual responsibility as publishers and educators creates an unprecedented collaborative environment among faculty and students, while teaching tomorrow's editors, designers, and marketers.

Outside of class, progress on book projects is carried forth by the AH Book Publishing Club, a co-curricular campus organization supported by Loyola University Maryland's Office of Student Activities.

Eclectic and provocative, Apprentice House titles intend to entertain as well as spark dialogue on a variety of topics. Financial contributions to sustain the press' work are welcomed. Contributions are tax deductible to the fullest extent allowed by the IRS.

To learn more about Apprentice House books or to obtain submission guidelines, please visit www.apprenticehouse.com.

Apprentice House
Communication Department
Loyola University Maryland
4501 N. Charles Street
Baltimore, MD 21210
Ph: 410-617-5265
info@apprenticehouse.com
www.apprenticehouse.com

CPSIA information can be obtained
at www.ICGtesting.com
Printed in the USA
LVHW082239240321
682407LV00002B/99